Faith for These End-Times

by
Jim Buller

TEACH Services, Inc.
PUBLISHING
www.TEACHServices.com

Copyright © 2012 Jim Buller & TEACH Services, Inc.
ISBN-13: 978-1-57258-807-3 (Paperback)
ISBN-13: 978-1-57258-808-0 (Hardback)
ISBN-13: 978-1-57258-809-7 (Epub)
ISBN-13: 978-1-57258-810-3 (Kindle/Mobi)

Library of Congress Control Number: 2012937343

Published by

TEACH Services, Inc.
P U B L I S H I N G
www.TEACHServices.com

Table of Contents

4

Introduction

"Without faith it is impossible to please Him" (Heb. 11:6).

"Our greatest need is faith in God"
(Testimonies for the Church, vol. 7, p. 211).

"The season of distress and anguish before us will require a faith that can endure weariness, delay, and hunger—a faith that will not faint though severely tried" (The Great Controversy, p. 621).

"Every failure on the part of the children of God is due to their lack of faith" (Patriarchs and Prophets, p. 657).

"When the Son of Man comes, will He really find faith on the earth?" (Luke 18:8).

For years, verses and quotations like the ones above have impressed me with the importance of faith —especially in our time. The realization that Eve's choice at the tree of the knowledge of good and evil was based on faith only added to that sense of importance. God and the serpent were essentially saying the exact opposite. "Don't eat the fruit; it is bad for you" versus "eat the fruit, it is good for you." Since Eve didn't know what would happen if she ate the fruit, her decision boiled down to: Who did she believe, and therefore, who did she trust? Every day we are each faced with essentially this same choice. Do we have faith in God, and what He tells us? Or do we believe some other voice? "Every failure ... *is* indeed due to [our] lack of faith."

Since a lack of faith caused everything to go wrong on the planet, it only makes sense that faith is the key to make things right again. No wonder, "Our greatest need is faith in God." How important then that we have a good working understanding of the subject of faith—"a faith that will not faint though severely tried."

The studies in this book grew out of my own research into the subject of faith. They took shape as lessons for my Bible classes. Encouraged by my students to share these lessons with the rest of the church, they later became articles in a more-or-less monthly e-mail newsletter I've been distributing called "Preparing to Stand." This book is an updated compilation of those articles containing my thoughts and ideas on faith.

The words faith, belief, and trust are closely related and have been used somewhat interchangeably throughout the book— "Faith includes not only belief but trust" (*Selected Messages,* book 1, p. 389).

"How to exercise faith should be made very plain" (*Education*, p. 253). My hope is that through this study you will gain a better understanding of how to exercise your faith and that you will determine in your own heart that when the Son of man comes, He will find faith in *you*.

—Jim Buller

"God calls for men who will prepare a people to stand in the great day of the Lord" (Gospel Workers 1915, p. 55).

Chapter 1

Four Steps to Great Faith

Since faith is such a key element in the Bible's teaching, it is probably safe to say that all the stories in the Bible are an illustration of faith. The stories either tell about someone who lived by faith or someone who was not faithful! From this perspective there is a definite pattern to the stories in the Bible. This pattern is easily seen in the story of the centurion and his servant.

> And a certain centurion's servant, who was dear to him, was sick and ready to die. So when he heard about Jesus, he sent elders of the Jews to Him, pleading with Him to come and heal his servant. And when they came to Jesus, they begged Him earnestly, saying that the one for whom He should do this was deserving, "for he loves our nation, and has built us a synagogue."
>
> Then Jesus went with them. And when He was already not far from the house, the centurion sent friends to Him, saying to Him, "Lord, do not trouble Yourself, for I am not worthy that You should enter under my roof. Therefore I did not even think myself worthy to come to You. But say the word, and my servant will be healed. For I also am a man placed under authority, having soldiers under me.

> And I say to one, 'Go,' and he goes; and to another, 'Come,' and he comes; and to my servant, 'Do this,' and he does it."
>
> When Jesus heard these things, He marveled at him, and turned around and said to the crowd that followed Him, "I say to you, I have not found such great faith, not even in Israel!" And those who were sent, returning to the house, found the servant well who had been sick (Luke 7:2-10).

This centurion didn't just have faith, he had "great faith!" So let's analyze the story to find out what this great faith is and how we can have it. To begin with, the first thing we notice about the centurion is that his servant is sick. He recognizes that he needs help. This is significant, because Laodicea, symbolic of the church in the last days, does not recognize its need (Rev. 3:17). If we are to have great faith, the first thing we must do is to *recognize our need*.

The second thing, or step as we will call it, is what the centurion did about his need—he took it to Jesus. But it is also important to notice his attitude as he comes to Jesus, especially as we contrast it with the attitude of the elders of the Jews in the story. He says, "I am not worthy." He is humble in his request. His statement about his relationship to authority also shows that he is submissive. And he trusts that Jesus will do what needs to be done. Therefore, the second step is to *take our need to Jesus* with an attitude of humility, submissiveness, and trust.

Where he asks Jesus to just "say the word," we find the third step. Although the centurion may not have known a lot about Jesus, he recognized one thing—when Jesus said something, it happened! There was *power* in Jesus' word. This reminds us of the old memory verse, "By the word of the LORD the heavens were made, and all the host of them by the breath of His mouth.... For He spoke, and it was done; He commanded, and it stood fast" (Ps. 33:6, 9). The centurion was confident that if Jesus said the word, his servant would be healed. So the third step is to *obtain the word of God regarding our situation*.

After the messengers obtained the word, they returned to the house and found the servant well. The fourth step then is to *act in harmony with the word of God*.

In summary, the four steps to great faith are as follows:

1. Recognize our need
2. Take our need to Jesus with an attitude of humility, submissiveness, and trust
3. Obtain the word of God regarding our situation, while we recognize the creative power of God's word
4. Act in harmony with the word of God

These four steps are also easily recognized in the story of Naaman the leper in 2 Kings 5:1-19. Naaman's story is an even better example of the importance of the fourth step, acting in harmony with the word of God.

Naaman recognized his need—he had leprosy! He took his need to Jesus via the prophet Elisha. He obtained the word of God regarding his situation with the instructions to go wash in the Jordan River seven times. However, the thought of washing in the muddy Jordan River made him angry, and he was reluctant to act in harmony with the word of God. But as he calmed down and listened to the advice of his servants, he went to the river, washed, and was healed.

Both of these stories teach us that God is interested in much more than just working miracles. He uses the opportunities created by our needs to teach us important lessons. Lessons that will make us better people in the long run. For example, Naaman needed to learn lessons in humility and submission, and the need to wash—even if in a muddy river—because leprosy is frequently associated with a lack of personal cleanliness.

To those of us who are weary and frustrated trying to meet our own needs, Jesus gives the invitation, "Come to Me, all you who labor and are heavy laden, and I will give you rest. Take My yoke upon you and learn from Me, for I am gentle and lowly in heart, and you will find rest for your souls. For My yoke is easy and My burden is light" (Matt. 11:28-30).

As you recognize needs in your own life, humbly and submissively take them to Jesus. Recognize the power of His Word, and find out what the Bible has to say about the situation you are in. Claim His promises, fulfill any conditions, and trust in Him to make it happen. Like the psalmist said, "I will cry out to God Most High, to God who performs all things for me" (Ps. 57:2). Bring your life into harmony with the Word to cooperate with what God is trying to do in your life. God wants to provide for all our needs in a way that will be best, not only for us but for everyone and everything around us, but we have to play our part by cooperating with His plan.

Look for the promises of God and hold on to them, having faith that God will do as He says He will do: "You open Your hand and satisfy the desire of every living thing" (Ps. 145:16); "And my God shall supply all your need according to His riches in glory by Christ Jesus" (Phil. 4:19).

Chapter 2

Jacob's Faith for Jacob's Time of Trouble

As we live by faith, following the four steps outlined in the first chapter, we are sometimes brought into trying circumstances. Jacob's experience in Genesis 31-33 is an excellent illustration of this. It also provides us with a glimpse of what our experience will be like during the time of trouble.

In the first part of Genesis 31, Jacob's brothers-in-laws complain that he has become wealthy at their expense, and Laban, his father-in-law, is not favorable toward him anymore. Jacob *recognizes his need* for help in this situation. Although it is not specifically mentioned at this point in the story, it is safe to conclude that Jacob took his need to God in prayer, especially when we realize who Jacob has become at this point in his life, which is evident from what he does later in the story.

We find that God answers his prayer, as He tells him, "Return to the land of your fathers and to you family, and I will be with you" (verse 3). Here he *obtains the word of God regarding the situation*. So, after making the necessary plans and preparations, Jacob and his family set out for Canaan—thus he *acted according to the word of God.* And so we see that Jacob is living by faith.

However, we find an interesting complication as we read on in the story. As a result of living by faith, following the four steps, Jacob runs into trouble. When he arrives in Canaan, messengers report that Esau is "coming to meet you, and four hundred men are with him" (Gen. 32:6). Esau, Jacob's twin brother, is evidently still angry about the loss of His birthright through Jacob's trickery (Gen. 27). At that time, Jacob had to flee for his life, and it seems that Esau is still bent on revenge and intends to attack Jacob's caravan.

Can you imagine the temptations Satan must have hurled at Jacob at this point? He probably reminded him of his past mistakes and reviewed the recent events with comments such as "You trusted God, did you? You've tried this living by faith thing, and just look at all the trouble it's gotten you into! And now your loved ones are in danger too!"

Isn't this similar to the way he tempts us? When we first think about following Jesus, he tries to discourage us by saying, "If you give your life to God, be sure to think about what He's going to have you do, and the things He won't let you do! Do you realize all the problems, anxieties, and lack of fulfillment you are going to experience?" Then later on, as we encounter difficult situations, he comes along and insinuates, "This is all the result of following Jesus. You are experiencing what it's really like to live by faith. You had better give up on following God and just get what you can out of life."

But Jacob did not give in to the devil's suggestions! He continued to live by faith, taking this new need to the Lord. Notice his attitude and how he claimed God's promises as he prayed.

> Then Jacob said, "O God of my father Abraham and God of my father Isaac, the LORD who said to me, 'Return to your country and to your family, and I will deal well with you': I am not worthy of the least of all the mercies and of all the truth which

You have shown Your servant; for I crossed over this Jordan with my staff, and now I have become two companies. Deliver me, I pray, from the hand of my brother, from the hand of Esau; for I fear him, lest he come and attack me and the mother with the children. For You said, 'I will surely treat you well, and make your descendants as the sand of the sea, which cannot be numbered for multitude'" (Gen. 32:9-12).

Jacob comes to God with the same attitude of humility, submissiveness, and trust as the centurion. Jacob admits that he is not worthy of God's help, yet he reminds God that he is in this situation as the result of following His leading and that He has promised to be with him and "deal well" with him.

That night, as Jacob goes out alone to pray, a Man appears, and the two of them wrestle through the night. At daybreak He touches Jacob's hip socket, causing it to go out of joint. In spite of the pain, Jacob realizes that this Man is a heavenly Messenger. As the Messenger tries to leave, Jacob hangs on, saying, "I will not let You go unless You bless me!" (Gen. 32:26). God blessed Jacob there, and with God's assurance and blessing, Jacob now can face Esau.

That night God also changed Esau's heart. The next day, "Esau ran to meet him, and embraced him, and fell on his neck and kissed him, and they wept" (Gen. 33:4). The brothers are reconciled and reunited. Esau is no longer resentful, and they part in peace.

In our own experience, as a result of living by faith and acting on the Word of God, we may sometimes find ourselves in difficult situations. Satan tempts us to give up, claiming that living God's way, by faith, has caused these impossible problems. However, these trials are actually a test of our faith, and they are calculated to result in spiritual endurance and steadfastness (James 1:2, 3). Instead of giving in to Satan's suggestions, may we be like Jacob and continue to live by faith, taking the new needs of our difficult situations and impossible problems to God, saying, "I will not let You go unless You bless me!"

Jeremiah 30:5-7 describes a troublous time ahead. Verse 7 says, "Alas! For that day is great, so that none is like it; and it is the time of Jacob's trouble, but he shall be saved out of it." During the great time of trouble, as a result of following God's Word, His people will find themselves in a tremendous crisis. They will not be able to buy or sell, and eventually it will be decreed that they should be killed (Rev. 13:15-17). This coming period of earth's history is often referred to as "the time of Jacob's trouble," no doubt to remind us of Jacob's experience.

Like Jacob, God has promised to be with us and deliver us. He allows trials to come our way so we will have the opportunity to learn that we can trust in Him. Through the experiences we have now, He wants us to gain the assurance of His presence and ability to deliver us from our difficulties. By learning now to habitually live by faith, we will be able to endure the trials of the time of trouble. May we make Jacob's experience our own and develop a faith that can say, regardless of the circumstance, "I will not let You go unless You bless me!"

Chapter 3

What Is the "Work" of Faith?

"The season of distress and anguish before us will require a faith that can endure weariness, delay, and hunger—a faith that will not faint though severely tried" (*The Great Controversy*, p. 621). After reading statements like this, many of us realize our need for more faith—the type of faith that can get us through the end-times. And like the disciples, we pray, "Lord, 'Increase our faith'" (Luke 17:5).

But exactly what is this type of faith? What does it look like? James 2:18 says, "Show me your faith without your works, and I will show you my faith by my works." But how can we tell if what we are doing, our "work," is being done in faith?

To illustrate this question, let's imagine living in Noah's time, and let's say there was a somewhat eccentric person who heard Noah preach. As he thought about what Noah was saying, he decided that building a boat was actually a pretty good idea. If there was a flood, he would be safe, and whether or not there was a flood, he could make lots of money doing commerce on the high seas. So he starts building a boat. From simply a casual glance, he and Noah look like a couple of "crazies" building their boats. Yet, one is acting in faith, whereas the other isn't. How can we tell the difference?

The answer is in the Bible's stories about faith. As was

presented in a previous chapter, the stories of the centurion with a sick servant (Luke 7:1-10) and Captain Naaman (2 Kings 5) help to outline four steps to having great faith:

1. Recognizing our need
2. Taking our need to Jesus with an attitude of humility, submissiveness, and trust
3. Obtaining the word of God regarding our situation, while we recognize the creative power of God's word
4. Acting in harmony with the word of God

Noah's experience also follows this same pattern. Genesis 6:9 tells us that "Noah walked with God." One day God told him of His plans to send a flood to destroy the earth because of its wickedness. Noah no doubt recognized his need to be saved from the coming destruction—step #1. He was already talking with God about this need so he had step #2 covered. As God told him, "Make yourself an ark" (Gen. 6:14), he obtained the word—step #3. Acting on the word, he went to work and built the ark—step #4.

And the record states, "By faith Noah, being divinely warned of things not yet seen, moved with godly fear, prepared an ark for the saving of his household" (Heb. 11:7). Noah acted on the word of God. He built the ark as a result of, and according to, God's instructions. The other boat builder in our imaginary story was building as a result of leaning on his own understanding (Prov. 3:5) rather than as a result of, or according to, God's instructions. This is how we can tell the difference between who is acting by faith and who is not.

In the same way, nowadays there are many people preparing for some version of an "The-End-Of-The-World-As-We-Know-It" scenario. Unfortunately, most of them are probably leaning on their own understanding, and not acting in faith. These people have a lot of different angles on country living and wilderness survival that are not necessarily according to God's Word. Although we may be able to learn some valuable skills and even some worthwhile concepts from these people, we need to be careful to "filter" what we learn from them. They may recognize the need to prepare, but they are not necessarily humbly and submissively taking this need to Jesus, nor are they searching for what the Word of God has to say on the subject. They are leaning on their own understanding rather than acting according to the Word. Therefore, they are not acting by faith.

On the other hand, God has given us warnings and instructions in the prophecies regarding what to prepare for and how to go about preparing for the end-times. To be acting by faith we must study these things so we can be sure that what we are doing is according to God's Word. If there were other boat builders in Noah's day, they surely did not make it through the flood. In the same way, only those who are truly acting in faith, that is, according to God's Word, will be able to endure to the end and be saved (Matt. 24:13). May we humbly and submissively search the Word and faithfully act on it in all areas of our lives.

Chapter 4

Abraham's Belief or the Demon's Belief?

Acts 16:31 sounds simple enough, "Believe on the Lord Jesus Christ, and you will be saved." However, in English we use the word "believe" in two very different ways, and if we don't recognize the distinction, we could end up on the wrong side of things—even though we might think we have a saving "belief."

Fortunately, in the second chapter of James both of the ways we use the word "believe" are described within just a few verses of each other. The first is in verse 19. It says, "You believe that there is one God. You do well. Even the demons believe and tremble!" The second is in verse 23. It says, "And the Scripture was fulfilled which says, 'Abraham believed God, and it was accounted to him for righteousness.' And he was called the friend of God."

Although the demons "believe," it is not accounted to them as righteousness, nor are they "friends" of God—they are in fact His enemies. They will not be "saved" because of *their* "belief." So this must not be the type of belief that is spoken of in Acts 16:31 quoted above. On the other hand, Abraham's belief *was* "accounted to him for righteousness. And he was called the friend of God." Abraham will be saved because of his belief.

So what's the difference? Notice what it is that the demons believe. They simply believe that God exists. They know and, therefore, believe the facts and the truths about God—which is more than what many humans believe. Thus, it is obviously not enough to just believe that there *is* a God or to just believe the various biblical truths for that matter, as the demons also believe that much! Please don't misunderstand me here; it is important to believe that God exists and to believe the many biblical truths, but we must not stop there, or we will be no better off than the demons.

Hebrew 11:6 is very helpful at this point. It says, "But without faith it is impossible to please Him, for he who comes to God must believe that He is, and that He is a rewarder of those who diligently seek Him." We must not only believe that He is—the facts about God—we must also believe "that He is a rewarder of those who diligently seek Him." The last couple words of this verse bring to mind Matthew 6:33: "But seek first the kingdom of God and His righteousness, and all these things shall be added unto you."

Abraham not only believed the facts about God, he believed *in* God. That is he believed in and wanted to be a part of what God and His kingdom are all about. Therefore, the chief pursuit of his life was "seeking first the kingdom of God." Both in his personal life and in the world around him, his purpose in life was to advance God's kingdom.

So what is God's kingdom all about? We will explore this in depth in chapters 6 and 7, so we will keep things simple for now. When Jesus called His disciples, He told them, "Follow *Me*." We need to be willing to let go of our agenda and humbly accept Jesus as our Leader and King—acknowledge Him in all our ways and let Him direct our paths (Prov. 3:5). Jesus also told us, "A new commandment I give to you … that you also love one another" (John 13:34). God's kingdom is all about love. Since we have been born as selfish sinners, we need to be willing to let Him change our selfishness into an unselfish love that will express itself in service to others (1 John 4:7, 8; Ezekiel 36:26, 27; Matthew 25:31-46).

Abraham believed it was worth it to "seek *first* the kingdom of

God and His righteousness" (Matt. 6:33). He felt that it would be better to follow God and serve Him by benefitting others than to pursue his own agenda. *This* is what Abraham believed, and therefore, *this* is what he did. *This* is what a saving belief, or a saving faith, is all about. Dear reader, "Examine yourselves as to whether you are in the faith" (2 Cor. 13:5). Do you have Abraham's type of belief? Or do you have the demons' type of belief, simply assenting mentally to the truths and facts about God without surrendering to His leadership or allowing the Holy Spirit to change your selfishness into unselfish love and service to God and others?

Chapter 5

Something Better— The Faith of Hebrews 11

When thinking about a definition for faith, many of us immediately go to Hebrews 11:1 which says, "Now faith is the substance of things hoped for, the evidence of things not seen." This *is* a valid scriptural definition. However, knowing the importance of faith, Satan works to lay his traps.

For instance, what is the "substance of things hoped for"? If we are content to simply answer, "faith," we may set ourselves up for some shallow circular thinking that doesn't really leave us with an adequate working definition for faith. If faith is simply the "substance of things hoped for," and if "the substance of things hoped for" is just faith, where does that leave us?

This type of circular thinking reminds me of a talk I once heard about creation versus evolution. The speaker told of a visit he had made to a geological site. While taking the tour, the guide informed the group that a particular strata of rock was "fifty million years old." (I may not have my numbers exactly right here, but you'll get the point.) Someone asked the guide how they knew the rock was "fifty million years old," and he replied that they were able to determine this because the rock contained fossils of fifty-million-year-old organisms. Later, when the guide was asked how they knew the fossils were "fifty million years old," he replied, "Because these fossils are in fifty million year old rock." Let's be careful we are not content with this type of shallow thinking in regards to our faith.

Another trap Satan has laid is the popular message that "if you only believe hard enough it will happen." Whereas this is not correct theology, we have to admit that this idea does fit within a definition of faith that is simply "the substance of things hoped for." This message states that if I hope for something "hard enough" there will be a real "substance" to my hopes, and this is called faith in the popular media.

Please don't misunderstand me here. I'm not saying that there is anything wrong with Hebrews 11:1. We just need to be careful that we are not content with these types of shallow "understandings" of what faith is all about. We need to dig deeper. And as with many cases in Scripture, this is easily done by reading the context of the verse.

The verses following Hebrews 11:1 talk about different men and women in the Bible who lived "by faith." Much can be learned about faith from their stories. But for the sake of time, we will skip through them and go directly to where the author of Hebrews summarizes what is to be learned from their experiences. He says,

> These all died in faith, not having received the promises, but having seen them afar off were assured of them, embraced them and confessed that they were strangers and pilgrims on the earth. For those who say such things declare plainly that they seek a homeland. And truly if they had called to mind that country from which they had come out, they would have had opportunity to return. But now they desire a better, that is, a heavenly country. Therefore God is not ashamed to be called their God, for He has prepared a city for them (Heb. 11:13-16).

"These all died in faith, not having received the promises." What promises? From the context here, it is obviously referring to God's promises of a better life in a better world. Notice that it says these great men and women of faith "were assured" of these promises and "embraced them." They literally grabbed hold of God's promises and held them tight.

Notice also that they "confessed that they were strangers and pilgrims on the earth." This world was not their home. They were seeking a heavenly homeland. Which reminds us of Matthew 6:33: "Seek first the kingdom of God and His righteousness, and all these things shall be added to you." The chief pursuit in the lives of these great men and women of faith was not the things of this world. It was "the kingdom of God and His righteousness."

Hebrews 11:15 states, "And truly if they had called to mind that country from which they had come out, they would have had opportunity to return." This statement reminds us of the experience of Abraham, who left his home and connections in the East, obeying the call to go to a place he was unfamiliar with. (His story was listed along with the Bible stories referenced earlier in Hebrews 11.)

This sentence also reminds us of a dream Ellen White had of a group of people heading up a path that continued to grow narrower and steeper as they went along (*Testimonies for the Church,* vol. 2, pp. 594-597, which is reprinted at the end of this chapter). They started out with heavily loaded wagons. But as the path grew narrower and steeper, they had to leave the wagons behind and continue on horseback. The path still continued to grow narrower and steeper, and they had to let go of the luggage they had brought with them on the horses. Further yet, they had to leave the horses behind to travel on foot. Still, the path grew narrower and steeper, and they ended up traveling barefoot, taking even their shoes and socks off. Finally the path ended altogether, and they swung across a chasm on cords of faith to "a beautiful field of green grass." The fifth paragraph of this story is highly significant. It says:

> We then thought of those who had not accustomed
> themselves to privations and hardships. Where were
> such now? They were not in the company. At every
> change some were left behind, and those only re-
> mained who had accustomed themselves to endure
> hardships. The privations of the way only made
> these more eager to press on to the end (p. 595).

"At every change some were left behind." Every time it was
necessary to leave something behind in order to keep going up
the path, there were those who took their "opportunity to return."
The sacrifice was too great. Rather than "embrace" the promises,
they chose to hang on to the "luggage." (For the rest of the chapter, we will use "luggage" to represent all the things that must be
left behind in order to continue on up the path.)

This brings us to the subject of worship and values and the
phrase in Hebrews 11:16 that says, "now they desire a *better*, that
is, a heavenly country." The root idea of "worship" is the concept
of "worth." The whole issue revolves around what we believe is of
value. What is worth it? Which is better? This raises a very important question. Is it worth it to let go of the "luggage" in order to
stay on the path toward what God has promised? At each stage of
our journey, we are faced with this question. Will we "embrace"
God's promises or hang onto the "luggage"?

Isaiah 55:8, 9 tells us, "'For My thoughts are not your thoughts,
nor are your ways My ways,' says the LORD. 'For as the heavens
are higher than the earth, so are My ways higher than your ways,
and My thoughts than your thoughts.'" And Galatians 5:17 says,
"For the flesh lusts against the Spirit, and the Spirit against the
flesh; and these are contrary to one another, so that you do not do
the things that you wish."

Are we willing to give up our own way of thinking and doing
and even the things we *want* for ourselves to be able to follow
the path God has laid out for us? Are we willing to let go of the
things that take up our time and resources and which keep us from

serving those whom God has called us to serve, things that might even be good in themselves, yet get in the way of our ministry? Is it worth it to hang on to these things? Or is it better to let go of them in order to keep traveling up the narrow path? Depending on what is most important to us, we will let go of either one or the other. Those who "embrace" the promises and keep going up the path do so because they believe that what God has to offer is "better" than any and everything else. Those who never start up the path or "return" after traveling a certain distance think something else is of more value.

As we think about this concept of following God on the narrow path, or turning back, let's consider a story in John 6. At the beginning of the chapter, Jesus feeds the five thousand. The people recognize that He must be the Messiah and are ready to take Him by force to make Him king. In order to defuse the situation, Jesus sends the disciples in the boat across the lake while He dismisses the people. Then He goes up on the mountain to pray (see also *The Desire of Ages* chapters 40 and 41). Later, a storm comes up, and Jesus walks out to the boat on the water. Once He gets into the boat, they are immediately at their destination on the far shore.

The next day when the people find Jesus and hear about the events of that night they become even more excited. Jesus knows they are going to try to make Him king again. And because that would be counterproductive to His overall mission, He tells them what His kingdom is all about—that it is first of all a spiritual kingdom, and that it will involve sacrificing worldly values (verses 26-65). As a result, the people realize Jesus is not going to be the type of king *they* want, and "from that time many of His disciples went back and walked with Him no more" (verse 66). They took their "opportunity to return." Things were so bad that "Jesus said to the twelve, 'Do you also want to go away?'" (verse 67).

"But Simon Peter answered Him, 'Lord, to whom shall we go? You have the words of eternal life'" (verse 68). In spite of all that was going on, much of which didn't even make sense to him, Peter believed that if he were to let go of Jesus what else would there be? To him, Jesus was everything, and His gift of eternal life was "better" than anything the world had to offer. Therefore, he was willing to give up his personal desires and opinions and humbly surrender to God's way. He chose to trust God, not lean on his own understanding (Prov. 3:5), and stay with Jesus on the narrow upward path.

Peter's comment, "You have the *words* of eternal life," also bring us to another important understanding about faith. Romans 10:17 tells us, "Faith comes by hearing ... the word of God." Thus, it is the promises contained in God's Word that are "the substance of things hoped for, the evidence of things not seen." Faith "embraces" these promises and, when necessary, lets go of any "luggage" that keeps us from continuing on up the path of faith. This kind of faith will dramatically affect our values, the choices we make, and the way we live.

Dear reader, do you believe that what God has for you is "better"? Is it *worth it* to let go of the comforts, conveniences, and approval of this world? Is it even *worth it* to let go of our own opinions, ideas, and desires? Is a life of self denial and service *worth* God's promise of eternal life in the earth made new? These are all questions we will each have to answer for ourselves. May we, along with the other faithful witnesses of Hebrews 11, answer "yes."

- - - - - - - - - - - - - - - - - - - -

"An Impressive Dream"

"While at Battle Creek in August, 1868, I dreamed of being with a large body of people. A portion of this assembly started out prepared to journey. We had heavily loaded wagons. As we journeyed, the road seemed to ascend. On one side of this road was a deep precipice; on the other was a high, smooth, white wall, like the hard finish upon plastered rooms.

"As we journeyed on, the road grew narrower and steeper. In

some places it seemed so very narrow that we concluded that we could no longer travel with the loaded wagons. We then loosed them from the horses, took a portion of the luggage from the wagons and placed it upon the horses, and journeyed on horseback.

"As we progressed, the path still continued to grow narrow. We were obliged to press close to the wall, to save ourselves from falling off the narrow road down the steep precipice. As we did this, the luggage on the horses pressed against the wall and caused us to sway toward the precipice. We feared that we should fall and be dashed in pieces on the rocks. We then cut the luggage from the horses, and it fell over the precipice. We continued on horseback, greatly fearing, as we came to the narrower places in the road, that we should lose our balance and fall. At such times a hand seemed to take the bridle and guide us over the perilous way.

"As the path grew more narrow, we decided that we could no longer go with safety on horseback, and we left the horses and went on foot, in single file, one following in the footsteps of another. At this point small cords were let down from the top of the pure white wall; these we eagerly grasped, to aid us in keeping our balance upon the path. As we traveled, the cord moved along with us. The path finally became so narrow that we concluded that we could travel more safely without our shoes, so we slipped them from our feet and went on some distance without them. Soon it was decided that we could travel more safely without our stockings; these were removed, and we journeyed on with bare feet.

"We then thought of those who had not accustomed themselves to privations and hardships. Where were such now? They were not in the company. At every change some were left behind, and those only remained who had accustomed themselves to endure hardships. The privations of the way only made these more eager to press on to the end.

"Our danger of falling from the pathway increased. We pressed close to the white wall, yet could not place our feet fully upon the path, for it was too narrow. We then suspended nearly our whole weight upon the cords, exclaiming: 'We have hold from above! We have hold from above!' The same words were uttered by all the company in the narrow pathway. As we heard the sounds of mirth and revelry that seemed to come from the abyss below, we shuddered. We heard the profane oath, the vulgar jest, and low, vile songs. We heard the war song and the dance song. We heard instrumental music and loud laughter, mingled with cursing and cries of anguish and bitter wailing, and were more anxious than ever to keep upon the narrow, difficult pathway. Much of the time we were compelled to suspend our whole weight upon the cords, which increased in size as we progressed.

"I noticed that the beautiful white wall was stained with blood. It caused a feeling of regret to see the wall thus stained. This feeling, however, lasted but for a moment, as I soon thought that it was all as it should be. Those who are following after will know that others have passed the narrow, difficult way before them, and will conclude that if others were able to pursue their onward course, they can do the same. And as the blood shall be pressed from their aching feet, they will not faint with discouragement; but, seeing the blood upon the wall, they will know that others have endured the same pain.

"At length we came to a large chasm, at which our path ended. There was nothing now to guide the feet, nothing upon which to rest them. Our whole reliance must be upon the cords, which had increased in size until they were as large as our bodies. Here we were for a time thrown into perplexity and distress. We inquired in fearful whispers: 'To what is the cord attached?' My husband was just before me. Large drops of sweat were falling from his brow, the veins in his neck and temples were increased to double their usual size, and suppressed, agonizing groans came from his lips. The sweat was dropping from my face, and I felt such anguish as I had never felt before. A fearful struggle was before us. Should we fail here, all the difficulties of our journey had been experienced for nought.

"Before us, on the other side of the chasm, was a beautiful field of green grass, about six inches high. I could not see the sun; but bright, soft beams of light, resembling fine gold and silver, were resting upon this field. Nothing I had seen upon earth could compare in beauty and glory with this field. But could we succeed in reaching it? was the anxious inquiry. Should the cord break, we must perish. Again, in whispered anguish, the words were breathed: 'What holds the cord?' For a moment we hesitated to venture. Then we exclaimed: 'Our only hope is to trust wholly to the cord. It has been our dependence all the difficult way. It will not fail us now.' Still we were hesitating and distressed. The words were then spoken: 'God holds the cord. We need not fear.' These words were then repeated by those behind us, accompanied with: 'He will not fail us now. He has brought us thus far in safety.'

"My husband then swung himself over the fearful abyss into the beautiful field beyond. I immediately followed. And, oh, what a sense of relief and gratitude to God we felt! I heard voices raised in triumphant praise to God. I was happy, perfectly happy.

"I awoke, and found that from the anxiety I had experienced in passing over the difficult route, every nerve in my body seemed to be in a tremor. This dream needs no comment. It made such an impression upon my mind that probably every item in it will be vivid before me while my memory shall continue" (*Testimonies for the Church,* vol. 2, pp. 594-597).

Chapter 6

Do You Really Want to Go to Heaven?

Or Is That Just the Best Option?

It may seem simple enough to state in principle that we believe that what God has for us is better than whatever this world has to offer, but is this what we really believe? We would do well to heed Paul's advice to "examine yourselves as to whether you are in the faith" (2 Cor. 13:5).

Suppose it was possible to go and visit "Heaven," kind of like going to a theme park. So, as an average Christian family, you decide to go there for your next vacation. When the time comes, you drive to the town nearest the "park" and check into a motel for the night with plans to visit "Heaven" the next day. In the morning, after getting ready for the day, you all go out for breakfast. Then you drive to "Heaven," park in the parking lot, and walk to the gate. At the entrance booth you start to pay the fee, but an "attendant" (an angel) waves you on in with a big smile saying, "Jesus has already paid for you. Heaven is free."

"How nice!" you think. "At least this vacation won't cost an arm and a leg."

As you step inside, the air seems fresher and everything looks brighter. There are all kinds of beautiful flowers everywhere, and everyone looks so pleasant and happy. Just beyond the entrance is a kiosk with a map and posters that let you know where you can play with the tigers, swim with the dolphins, and ride an elephant. It also gives information about where you can meet Jesus and listen to a concert by the angel choir. There are instructional sessions with actual hands-on experiences about how to take care of various plants and animals, and there are presentations on practical Christian living and family relationships. It also shows where there are different exhibits on the wonders of the universe, and where you can even take flying lessons! So you begin to wander around and enjoy all the "attractions."

After a while you get hungry, so you look around for a concession stand, but you don't find any. So you ask one of the "attendants" where you and your family can get something to eat. The "attendant" says you can help yourself to the fruit and nuts on any of the trees or the seeds from many of the plants. With a bit of a question in our voice you say, "OK," and begin looking around at the trees. Sampling some of the fruit, you and your family find it to be the most delicious you have ever tasted!

Later that afternoon, even though the children are still having fun, you can tell they are starting to get tired. You begin wondering when the place closes, and seeing one of the "attendants" nearby, you ask him. He says you can stay as long as you like. If you want, you can sleep out under the trees or stay in one of the cabins, which to your surprise, he says is already reserved for your family. After asking him for directions, you head off to check out "your" cabin. When you get there, you find that it is nice, simply furnished, but you also notice that there is no television.

By now the children are hungry again, and you are too. The kids ask if they can go somewhere to get some "real food" and then go back to the motel. Out of curiosity, you ask if they have enjoyed their visit to "Heaven." They respond that they've liked it really well; they're just ready to do something else. Still curious, you ask them what they want to do back at the motel. They reply that they just want to watch TV and play the video games they've brought along.

So although you feel kind of strange, like something isn't quite the way it should be, you head for the car.

As you reach the exit, you notice Jesus standing there. He seems strangely sad as you thank Him and tell Him goodbye. As He watches you and your family exit through the gate, you think you notice a tear running down His cheek.

- - - - - - - - - - - - - - - - - - - -

Parents, I hope the message here is obvious. The idea for this chapter came from observing the reaction of my students to trips into nature over the last several years. Unfortunately, most children nowadays have had a lot of exposure to the media and very little exposure to nature. For several generations now one subtle message of our culture has been that nature is not "where it's at." As a result, most of us have a hard time appreciating, for any length of time, what God has created for us to enjoy—for eternity.

Please think seriously about this. How can we truly worship the Creator and keep the Sabbath—the memorial of Creation—if we don't appreciate, or possibly even ignore nature? Are we preparing ourselves to get tired of heaven simply by the way we live our day-to-day lives? Once the novelty has worn off, will we be bored for the rest of eternity? Is this what we are faithfully enduring the trials and sufferings associated with the Christian life for? It may seem simple enough to state in principle that we believe that what God has for us is better than whatever this world has to offer, but do we live our lives consistent with this belief?

Let's put it another way. When God created Adam and Eve, where did He put them? In the Garden of Eden. And what was outside of the garden? A vast world full of "nature." So they were essentially placed in the wilderness! And what did they do in the garden? Did they just wander around all day looking at the beauty, which is what most people nowadays do when they get out in nature? No. If this was all they did, how long would it have been until they were completely bored? Instead, Adam and Eve daily interacted with nature to get the things they needed similar to the way many native peoples have "lived off the land." Humans were created to be a part of the ecosystem rather than apart from it. This is the life the Creator intended for human beings to live!

Then after the flood where did God put His people again? As they came out of the ark, the earth was again one vast wilderness. God told them, "Be fruitful and multiply, and *fill the earth*" (Gen. 9:1). Humankind was to go out and live in this wilderness. But after a few generations the people said, "Let us build ourselves a city, and a tower ... let us make a name for ourselves, lest we be scattered over the face of the whole earth" (Gen. 11:4). It seems that God keeps putting people out in nature, and people keep building cities.

And after "the restoration of all things" (Acts 3:21), where will we be again? Back in the garden. So it is not surprising that as a part of our final preparation for heaven God puts us out in the country, and then in the wilderness for a while!

The question begs to be asked, "Is it possible to truly appreciate Jesus dying so we can live if we don't appreciate the life He intended for us to live?" That is, a life closely connected with the natural world He created for us to live in? After all, He didn't die so we could keep living the same disconnected life we always have. It was because of this disconnected life that He had to die in the first place!

If we don't appreciate what God has promised, will we "embrace" these promises (Heb. 11:13)? Will we be willing to let go of the "luggage" in order to keep on the upward path of faith and swing over to the "beautiful field of green grass" if we don't appreciate the "grass" (*Testimonies for the Church*, vol. 2, pp. 594-597)? Will it be worth it for us to let go of things we do value for something we only value in principle?

No wonder we have been told in *Testimonies for the Church* that "those who sacrifice simplicity to fashion, and shut themselves away from the beauties of nature, cannot be spiritually minded" (vol. 2, p. 584). Notice that it doesn't say we will just have *a hard time* being spiritually minded if we shut ourselves away from nature, it says that we "*cannot* be spiritually minded." If we close ourselves off from nature—it is impossible! No wonder Satan has arranged things in modern society in such a way that nature isn't even a part of most peoples reality anymore!

May we cooperate with God as He tries to bring us in touch with the natural world He has created for us to live in. Instead of listening to the messages of our modern culture and ignoring nature, or believing the false witness that nature is a scary place, may we prepare ourselves and our children to actually appreciate and enjoy living forever among the vast creations of God?

The following quotes by Ellen White provide great insight onto this topic:

> All who are under the training of God need the quiet hour for communion with their own hearts, with nature, and with God. In them is to be revealed a life that is not in harmony with the world, its customs, or its practices; and they need to have a personal experience in obtaining a knowledge of the will of God. We must individually hear Him speaking to the heart. When every other voice is hushed, and in quietness we wait before Him, the silence of the soul makes more distinct the voice of God. He bids us, "Be still, and know that I am God." Psalm 46:10. This is the effectual preparation for all labor for God. Amidst the hurrying throng, and the strain of life's intense activities, he who is thus refreshed will be surrounded with an atmosphere of light and peace. He will receive a new endowment of both physical and mental strength. His life will breathe out a fragrance, and will reveal a divine power that will reach men's hearts (*The Ministry of Healing*, p. 58).

While the Bible should hold the first place in the education of children and youth, the book of nature is next in importance. God's created works testify to His love and power (*Counsels to Parents, Teachers, and Students,* p. 185).

The whole natural world is designed to be an interpreter of the things of God (*Ibid.,* p. 186).

In the natural world, God has placed in the hands of the children of men the key to unlock the treasure house of His word. The unseen is illustrated by the seen; divine wisdom, eternal truth, infinite grace, are understood by the things that God has made (*Ibid.,* p. 187).

As we observe the things of the natural world, we shall be enabled, under the guiding of the Holy Spirit, more fully to understand the lessons of God's word. It is thus that nature becomes a key to the treasure house of the word (*Education,* p. 120).

In these lessons direct from nature, there is a simplicity and purity that makes them of the highest value. All need the teaching to be derived from this source. In itself the beauty of nature leads the soul away from sin and worldly attractions, and toward purity, peace, and God (*Christ's Object Lessons,* p. 24).

The Sabbath bids us behold in His created works the glory of the Creator. And it was because He desired us to do this that Jesus bound up His precious lessons with the beauty of natural things. On the holy rest day, above all other days, we should study the messages that God has written for us in nature (*Ibid.,* pp. 25, 26).

Nature and revelation alike testify of God's love. Our Father in heaven is the source of life, of wisdom, and of joy. Look at the wonderful and beautiful things of nature. Think of their marvelous adaptation to the needs and happiness, not only of man, but of all living creatures (*Steps to Christ*, p. 9).

Chapter 7

Harmony

At the end of creation week, "God saw everything that He had made, and indeed it was very good" (Gen. 1:31). Throughout the whole world everything was in harmony with God and with each other, for "God is not the author of disorder but of peace" (1 Cor. 14:33, margin).

But then Satan tempted Eve at the tree of the knowledge of good and evil. He told her that if she ate the fruit her "eyes [would] be opened," and she would "be like God, knowing good and evil" (Gen. 3:5). Like God, she would know what was good and what was bad and would be able to choose what was right and wrong—for herself. She would not need God to tell her what to do.

This same idea was a key element in Satan's own fall, for he had said, "I will be like the Most High" (Isa. 14:14). Like Satan, Adam and Eve chose to be their own "god," deciding for themselves what they should do or not do. And ever since, to one extent or another, the whole human race has been infected with this same notion that we don't need God to tell us what to do because we can decide what is best for ourselves. Today we still hear, and unfortunately yield, to the same tempting message that says, "You're intelligent. You're the one who really knows what is best for yourself. So, to find the most fulfillment in life, just follow your heart." In other words, you can do the best job at directing your own life since you are the only one who really knows what would be good or bad for yourself.

But what is the result of everyone choosing what is right and wrong for themselves? To illustrate this, let's think for a moment about what would happen if, although we are each doing whatever we think we should do, somehow we all decided to get together and sing. However, when we get together, each of us sings whatever song we think would be best. What would happen? It would be chaos! Or suppose we somehow all choose to sing the same song, but each of us decided for ourselves which key to sing in, what rhythm, and when we would start singing? It would still be chaos!

To avoid this chaos and confusion, we have a song leader or director to start everyone off on the same song, at the same time, in the same key, and with the same rhythm. And the result of everyone singing together can be beautiful and harmonious. Please note that it is not necessary for the song leader to be a bossy tyrant or for the singers to be mindless slaves for this to happen. In fact, many times the person who is acting as song leader doesn't even realize they are the ones leading—everyone just follows them, so we can sing together. For this type of harmony to exist, we must have two things: first, there needs to be someone who organizes or "directs traffic" so to speak; and second, everyone else involved must be willing to cooperate and follow this director's leading.

So, who is best qualified to be the "director" of the universe? The obvious answer is the Creator. No one else even comes close. No one else knows all the intricate needs and interactions of all things. This then brings us to the central question. "Is the Creator really organizing and directing things for everyone's best good?" Or to personalize the issue, "Can *I* trust God to do what is best for *me*?"

The choice Eve faced at the tree of the knowledge of good and evil centered around this very question. She had to choose—was she going to trust and follow God, or was she going to rely on her own understanding and do things her own way. And still today, probably several times every day, each one of us are faced with this same basic choice. Are we going to trust and follow God, or are we going to follow our own hearts and minds?

To help us answer this question in an intelligent manner, we need to ask another question. What is the overall principle behind God's organizational plan? We find the answer to this in John 15:1-8, where Jesus uses the example of a grape vine to describe this plan. He says:

> I am the true vine, and My Father is the vinedresser. Every branch in Me that does not bear fruit He takes away; and every branch that bears fruit He prunes, that it may bear more fruit.… Abide in Me, and I in you. As the branch cannot bear fruit of itself, unless it abides in the vine, neither can you, unless you abide in Me. I am the vine, you are the branches. He who abides in Me, and I in him, bears much fruit; for without Me you can do nothing. If anyone does not abide in Me, he is cast out as a branch and is withered; and they gather them and throw them into the fire, and they are burned.… By this My Father is glorified, that you bear much fruit; so you will be My disciples.

As a result of being connected with Him—that is, relying on His wisdom, trusting His provision, and following His plan—Jesus said we would "bear much fruit." But what does He mean by "bearing fruit"? It is both interesting and significant that Jesus chose fruit to illustrate His point. So let's think like a botanist for a minute and ask, "What do the different parts of a plant do for the plant they are growing on?" For the sake of simplicity, we will generalize plant parts to: roots, stems, leaves, and flowers which turn into fruit.

What do the roots do for the plant? They provide support and soak up water and soil nutrients. If the roots were to be cut off of the plant, it would literally fall over and die. Roots, therefore, are essential for the survival of the plant.

What do the stems do? They have vascular tissue that carries the water and nutrients around to the whole plant, and they provide a framework to hold the leaves out in the sunlight so they can do their job. Without the stems and branches, the plant would die. In fact, if just a strip of bark is cut off all the way around a tree (a practice called girding), it will kill the tree.

And the leaves? Through the process of photosynthesis, they use sunlight energy to turn water and carbon dioxide into sugar, making food for the plant. If the plant did not have any leaves, it would starve to death. So leaves, too, are essential for the survival of the plant.

Plants grow roots, stems, and leaves because they all perform vital functions for the survival of the plant. Without any one of them, the plant would die. Which brings us to the fruit. What does fruit do for the plant it is growing on? Nothing. A plant can grow very well without producing any fruit.

Because fruit does nothing for the plant it is growing on, it may seem strange that Jesus chose fruit to illustrate the result of being connected with Him. However, looking at the bigger picture we find that fruit is something the plant does, not for itself, but to *benefit others*. Fruit can be food for birds and animals. Fruit contains the seeds to start new plants. Fruit even benefits nonliving things, for if it just falls to the ground and decomposes, it at least enriches the soil.

Taking a look at nature, we also find that most plants put their whole life energy into bearing fruit. Take a healthy tomato plant for instance. Suppose we were to compare the weight of the tomato plant itself with the weight of all the tomatoes it produced. Which would weigh more? The tomatoes! This would definitely be true of watermelons! It is true of fruit trees too, when we consider all the fruit produced during the lifetime of the tree. Other plants, grains in particular, pour their whole life energy into producing fruit, something that does nothing for themselves, and then they die. Thus we find that plants exist for the purpose of benefitting others.

To the selfish way of thinking, this doesn't make sense, for another common message tells us, "Look out for yourself, because no one else is going to." But instead of looking out for themselves, plants literally pour their whole lives into benefitting others!

In spite of the effects of sin, plants still give us an excellent illustration of God's plan for all of creation. For even nonliving things like sunlight, air, water, dirt, and rocks exist to benefit others. So we find that everything was created to exist for the purpose of benefitting others. This is the Creator's overall organizational plan. And this is why Jesus said, as a result of our connection with Him, we would "bear *much fruit*." By following Him and living according to His principles, *we* will live to bless others.

There is another important point in John 15:4, 5 that we need to emphasize. Let's read it again.

> Abide in Me, and I in you. As the branch cannot bear fruit of itself, unless it abides in the vine, neither can you, unless you abide in Me. I am the vine, you are the branches. He who abides in Me, and I in him, bears much fruit; for without Me you can do nothing.

Fruit is borne *only* on a branch that is attached to the vine. If a branch is disconnected from the vine, it withers up and dies (John 15:6). Therefore, we are not expected to try to "bear fruit," or benefit others, on our own, or from our own resources. We can only be a benefit to others by being connected to the Source of all benefits and good things—the Creator Himself (Col. 1:16 and James 1:17).

Thus we find that God created everything in the universe to pass on the benefits it received as a result of maintaining its connection with Him. In the same way, as we maintain *our* connection with Him and fill our place in His plan, we too will bear some kind of "fruit" or pass along some benefit to the things around us. Because we "freely receive" from Him, we are able to "freely give" to others (Matt. 10:8). As we look around in nature, we find that all things, both living and nonliving, exist for the purpose of benefitting others. Blessings from God are passed on from one created thing to another. Each thing receives what it needs and then produces something that is useful to other things. For example, plants receive the soil nutrients and sunlight energy that animals cannot readily make use of, and then they produce fruits and vegetables that animals can use for food. The animals in turn do things to benefit plants, such as spreading seeds, fertilizing, thinning, and pruning.

God created the whole universe to be a huge interconnected network of benefit sharing. Instead of each thing just looking out for itself, everything exists to benefit others. Thus the needs of each individual are met by the abundant sharing of everything around it. This is God's overall organizational plan, and everything in the universe follows this plan—everything except demons and selfish humans.

The results of not following God's plan can easily be seen in the condition of our planet. In the beginning, "The Lord God took the man and put him in the garden of Eden to tend and keep it" (Gen. 2:15). And by extension, the human race, as it spread across the globe, was to take care of the whole world. However, instead of being a benefit to the earth, humans have come close to destroying it! No wonder sin has been confined to this planet.

Our lives, therefore, will have the greatest fulfillment when we occupy the position God has for us in His "network"—in His plan. Then we will be in the right place, at the right time, to receive all the blessings He sends our way, and we will also be able to pass on all the benefits He has planned for us to give to others. Only the Creator would be able to organize and maintain the harmony of a system as complicated as this. However, for this system to run smoothly, it is necessary for everyone and everything to stay connected to the Creator, to choose to fill their place in His plan, and to be willing to share.

Think for a moment about the intricate inner workings of a

windup clock. Because of the interconnectedness of all the different parts, if even one part were to stop functioning as it should, eventually the whole clock would stop working. In the same way, one selfish, uncooperative individual can potentially cause problems throughout the entire universe! When we choose to direct our own lives and do things our own way, we are not cooperating with the Creator's plan, nor are we filling our place in it. And as a result, we will not be where we need to be to receive the things God sends our way, (no wonder our needs are not met); nor will we be passing on the things God has planned for us to share with those around us, (no wonder the needs of others are not met). Thus the flow of benefits throughout the whole network is disrupted in the same way that one pebble thrown into a pond causes ever widening ripples that eventually reach the farthest shore. One of the reasons Christ died was to show the eventual extent of the ruin that is caused by being out of harmony with God's plan.

But more importantly, Christ's death is a demonstration of God's love. It shows that He too operates by the same principle of living to benefit others. Christ's death shows that He is willing to do whatever is necessary for the good of His creatures, even to the point of giving the ultimate gift —His own life! "But God demonstrates His own love toward us, in that while we were still sinners, Christ died for us" (Rom. 5:8). He died to show us that we really can trust Him. That in all His plans, He really is organizing and directing things for our best good. In fact, because of His infinite wisdom, power, and love, He can do a much better job of looking out for our needs and interests than we are able to do for ourselves.

God does not want us to just follow Him out of instinct, simply because we were programmed that way. He wants us to follow Him because we recognize that His way is best—best for us and best for everything else. Therefore, unlike the rest of creation, God made humans with the ability to choose whether to be a part of His plan or to go our own selfish way. One reason He did this is because from His perspective our intelligent choice to follow Him is the most valuable thing in the universe, as it is the one thing He cannot create.

Yes, "free choice," as it is called, opened the possibility for someone to go his or her own way—and then to deceive others into thinking that going their own way would be best. Therefore, as a part of His design in the creation of this earth, Christ also planned to come and die for those who may be deceived. He became the "Lamb *slain from the foundation of the world*" (Rev. 13:8). His death made the "plan of redemption" possible and provided the opportunity for us to be brought back into harmony with both Himself and the rest of His creation (Col. 1:19-23).

Since Adam and Eve, all of us have selfishly chosen to go our own way instead of following our Creator's plan. This choice has produced chaos and confusion, which has lead to unfulfilled needs. Like a broken clock or a disconnected branch, the inevitable result is dysfunction and death. But on the cross Jesus died in our place so that by cooperating with Him we could again live fulfilled, harmonious lives. He assures us, "I have come that they may have life, and that they may have it more abundantly" (John 10:10).

Love & Sharing	Pride & Selfishness
Choice (faith-trust-believe)	
God's Way	**Satan's Way**
"follow Me"/"bear fruit"	"do what you want to do"
order & harmony	chaos
fulfilled needs	unfulfilled needs
abundant life	death

But we cannot bring ourselves back into harmony anymore than a disconnected branch can reattach itself. Only the Creator can recreate this connection. All we can do is choose to cooperate with Him and be willing to give up our selfishness, trusting and allowing Him to do what needs to be done, both to reattach us to Himself and to strengthen our connection. So each day, and several times throughout the day, we should renew our choice to stay connected to Him, asking Him to keep the connection strong and to pour His life through us so we can be a benefit to others. If we ever find that we have yielded to the temptation to go our own way again, we simply need to recommit ourselves to Him and let Him reconnect us once more. "Now may the God of peace Himself sanctify you completely; and may your whole spirit, soul, and body be preserved blameless at the coming of our Lord Jesus Christ. He who calls you is faithful, who also will do it" (1 Thess. 5:23, 24).

To use a more modern illustration, God wants us to be like a garden hose. One end is connected to a faucet, and the other end has one of those squeeze-valves on it. The faucet represents our connection to God—the Source of all blessings. Water represents these blessings; and the squeeze-valve represents our choice to be selfish or unselfish.

In the same way that the purpose of a hose is to be a channel to carry water, our purpose is to be a channel to spread God's blessings. In order for water to flow out of the hose, the hose must be connected to the faucet, the faucet must be turned on, and the squeeze-valve must be open. In the same way, if we are to share God's blessings, we must be connected to Him, allow the Holy Spirit to flow through our lives, and have our "selfishness valve" open. As long as the hose is connected to the open faucet, it can spray water indefinitely without a risk of becoming empty itself. And if we allow ourselves to be a channel for God's blessings, our lives will also be full of blessings. We *can* "freely give" *because* we have "freely received."

If we are not connected to the Source, or if our relationship-faucet isn't "open," we may as well hang on to what we have.

Although by selfishly closing off the squeeze-valve in order to hold onto the water, it only stagnates, especially in the hot summer sun! The only way to continually be full of fresh clean water is to *let it flow*! Allowing water to flow out the end of the hose makes room for more fresh water to enter. Thus if we want more blessings in our lives, we must share what we have. We need to learn that it *is* safe to share because there is plenty more where that came from. We also need to develop habits of staying connected to the Source and keeping our relationship open.

To take this illustration one step further, like the stony ground in the parable of the sower, we can have things in our lives that obstruct the flow of God's blessing (Matt. 13:5, 6). These obstructions keep us from growing and bearing fruit. This would be represented by things getting inside the hose and blocking the flow of water.

We need to be willing to let go of these things. If we had a hose that was plugged and we were not able to unclog it, it would be useless, and we would throw it out. As Jesus said in John 15:2, "Every branch in Me that does not bear fruit He takes away; and every branch that bears fruit He prunes, that it may bear more fruit." As someone pointed out once, one way or the other we are going to get "cut." Either we will allow God to cut away the things that keep us from being fruitful, or we will get cut off as an unfruitful branch. Which brings us to the parable of the unfruitful fig tree in Luke 13:6-9.

> "A certain man had a fig tree planted in his vineyard, and he came seeking fruit on it and found none. Then he said to the keeper of the vineyard, 'Look, for three years I have come seeking fruit on this fig tree and find none. Cut it down; why does it use up the ground?' But he answered and said to him, 'Sir, let it alone this year also, until I dig around it and fertilize it. And if it bears fruit, well. But if not, after that you can cut it down.'"

The owner of the vineyard had planted the fig tree to bear figs. If it remained unfruitful year after year, he had a right to take it out. Why should it take up space if it was not going to fulfill its purpose. In the same way, God created us to bear fruit and be a blessing to others. But if in our selfishness we refuse to be fruitful, He has a right to cut us down, which is one reason why the wicked are destroyed in the end.

Unfortunately, our selfish human nature has twisted our thinking, and we don't really understand what unselfish love is, and we certainly can't trust the world's definition! As God says, "'My thoughts are not your thoughts, nor are your ways My ways,' says the Lord. 'For as the heavens are higher than the earth, so are My ways higher than your ways, and My thoughts than your thoughts'" (Isa. 55:8, 9). This is why God has given us the Bible with all its instructions, so we can know how to truly be loving and unselfish.

It is my prayer in writing this that you will understand God's love and wisdom and that you will recognize His willingness to do what is best for you, as well as for the rest of creation. May you also realize that following His way of sharing is better than our way of selfishness, chaos, and death. I pray that you will desire to fill your place in His plan and that you will choose to allow Him to get rid of your selfishness, so you can be reconnected and brought back into harmony with Himself and the rest of the universe.

The following quotations are shared to help round out the above ideas and encourage you as you choose to fill your place in God's plan.

> Trust in the Lord with all your heart, and lean not on your own understanding; in all your ways acknowledge Him, and He shall direct your paths. Do not be wise in your own eyes; fear the Lord and depart from evil (Prov. 3:5-7).

> In the beginning, God was revealed in all the works of creation. It was Christ that spread the heavens, and

laid the foundations of the earth. It was His hand that hung the worlds in space, and fashioned the flowers of the field. "His strength setteth fast the mountains." "The sea is His, and He made it." Psalm 65:6; 95:5. It was He that filled the earth with beauty, and the air with song. And upon all things in earth, and air, and sky, He wrote the message of the Father's love.

Now sin has marred God's perfect work, yet that handwriting remains. Even now all created things declare the glory of His excellence. There is nothing, save the selfish heart of man, that lives unto itself. No bird that cleaves the air, no animal that moves upon the ground, but ministers to some other life. There is no leaf of the forest, or lowly blade of grass, but has its ministry. Every tree and shrub and leaf pours forth that element of life without which neither man nor animal could live; and man and animal, in turn, minister to the life of tree and shrub and leaf. The flowers breathe fragrance and unfold their beauty in blessing to the world. The sun sheds its light to gladden a thousand worlds. The ocean, itself the source of all our springs and fountains, receives the streams from every land, but takes to give. The mists ascending from its bosom fall in showers to water the earth, that it may bring forth and bud (*The Desire of Ages*, pp. 20, 21).

Christ is our example. He gave his life as a sacrifice for us, and he asks us to give our lives as a sacrifice for others. Thus we may cast out the selfishness which Satan is constantly striving to implant in our hearts. This selfishness is death to all piety, and can be overcome only by manifesting love to God and to our fellow men. Christ will not permit one selfish person to enter the courts of heaven. No covetous person can pass through the pearly gates; for all covetousness is idolatry (*The Review and Herald,* July 11, 1899).

No outward observances can take the place of simple faith and entire renunciation of self. But no man can empty himself of self. We can only consent for Christ to accomplish the work. Then the language of the soul will be, Lord, take my heart; for I cannot give it. It is Thy property. Keep it pure, for I cannot keep it for Thee. Save me in spite of myself, my weak, unchristlike self. Mold me, fashion me, raise me into a pure and holy atmosphere, where the rich current of Thy love can flow through my soul (*Christ's Object Lessons*, p. 159).

Sin, that cost Adam beautiful Eden, exists everywhere in our world. Evil triumphs wherever God is not known or his character contemplated. We could not commit sin if we realized the presence of God, and thought upon his goodness, his love, and his compassion. Satan knows that if he can obscure the vision so that the eye of faith cannot behold God, there will be no barrier against sin. It is necessary to know God in order to be attracted to him. And the perception of his image as represented in Christ changes the sinner's views of evil. The shadow of Satan obscures the character of Jesus and of God; but if we by faith gain a knowledge of God, and hold steadfastly to Jesus, we shall be changed. In Jesus is manifested the character of the Father, and the sight of him attracts. It softens and subdues, and ceases not to transform the character, until Christ is formed within, the hope of glory. The human heart that has learned to behold the character of God may become, under the influence of the Holy Spirit, like a sacred harp, sending forth divine melody (*The Signs of the Times*, August 24, 1891).

The strongest argument in favor of the gospel is a loving and lovable Christian (*The Ministry of Healing*, p. 470).

Chapter 8

The Faith of Jesus

"Here is the patience of the saints, here are those who keep the commandments of God and the faith of Jesus" (Rev. 14:12). This comment comes at the close of the three angels' messages—the final end-time messages to everyone on the planet. Its position, just after the third message, is especially significant. In part, this third message states, "If anyone worships the beast and his image, and receives his mark on his forehead or on his hand, he himself shall also drink of the wine of the wrath of God, which is poured out full strength into the cup of His indignation" (Rev. 14:9, 10). The issue of worshiping the beast and its image and receiving the mark of the beast comes to a head during the time just before Jesus comes. For good reason, this time is known as the great time of trouble or the great tribulation (Dan. 12:1; Matt. 24:21).

Revelation 13 tells us more about this issue. Verse 8 says, "All who dwell on the earth will worship him [the beast]." So everyone "whose names have not been written in the Book of Life of the Lamb slain from the foundation of the world" will worship the beast! Then verse 11 tells us about another beast who comes up with "two horns like a lamb" but speaks "like a dragon." This second beast forces "the earth and those who dwell in it to worship the first beast" by making an Image of the first beast and causing "as many as would not worship the image of the beast to be killed" (verses 12 and 15).

This creates a dilemma because, as noted earlier, the third

angel's message states that those who worship the beast and his image will "drink of the wine of the wrath of God" (Rev. 14:8). Revelation 15 tells us more about the wine of God's wrath. There, "seven angels" are depicted as "having the seven last plagues, for in them the wrath of God is complete" (verse 1). These angels are given "seven golden bowls full of the wrath of God" (verse 7). So the wine of the wrath of God is the seven last plagues, which will be poured out on everyone who worships the beast and its image or receives its mark.

But that is not all. The last verse in Revelation 15 states that "the temple was filled with smoke from the glory of God and from His power, and no one was able to enter the temple till the seven plagues of the seven angels were completed" (verse 8). In the Old Testament symbolic service, the temple was where people's sins were forgiven. So if no one will be able to enter the heavenly temple, this means that from the time just before the plagues are poured out no more sins will be forgiven. Therefore, probation, or the time of grace, ends just before the plagues. In other words, those who worship the beast and his image and receive the mark of the beast essentially commit the unpardonable sin, receive the seven last plagues, and are eternally lost.

Thus during the coming time of trouble or great tribulation, we will all be faced with the choice (1) to either worship the beast and its image and receive the mark of the beast, but in so doing commit the unpardonable sin, have the plagues poured out on us, and be eternally lost; or (2) stay true to God by refusing to worship the beast or its image or receiving the mark and be sentenced to death by these worldly powers. This will indeed call for patient endurance on the part of the saints who continue to "keep the commandments of God and the faith of Jesus!" (Rev. 14:12). The need for patient endurance through this trial is easy to understand, as is the call to continue keeping the commandments of God. But what exactly is meant by "the faith of Jesus."

In English, we have two ways to describe possession. We can

either say, for example, this is John's Bible, or we could say this is the Bible of John. (Other languages don't have the apostrophe "s" possessive form as we do in English, such as in Spanish it is only possible to say *la Biblia de Juan* [the Bible of John].) Therefore, in English "the faith of Jesus" could also be expressed as "Jesus' faith." Both would describe the faith that Jesus possesses. So this comment, connected with the third angel's message, lets us know that in order to make it through this final trial we will need to have the same type of faith that Jesus possessed. But what exactly is this type of faith? And how can we have it?

James 1:2, 3 tells us, "My brethren, count it all joy when you fall into various trials, knowing that the testing of your faith produces patience." Thus our trials and temptations are really a test of our faith. So, since we will need Jesus' faith to make it through the great tribulation, which will be our greatest trial, where can we expect to find the greatest demonstration of His faith? The answer must be at His greatest trial!

It was in the Garden of Gethsemane that Jesus made the decision to go through with the crucifixion. In His humanity He really didn't want to be misrepresented and condemned in court, mocked and beaten, nailed to the cross, and left there to die. This was evident from the first part of His prayer, as in anguish He said, "O My Father, if it is possible, let this cup pass from Me" (Matt. 26:39). But, rather than choosing what He wanted, He added, "nevertheless, not as I will, but as You will" (Ibid., see also verses 42 and 44). This prayer expresses a complete and total surrender to the Father's wisdom and will. In faith He actually surrendered even His power of choice, as He essentially prayed, "Not what I would choose but, based on Your wisdom and love, what You choose!" The faith of Jesus, therefore, is a complete faith in the Father that results in a total surrender to His will. This is the same type of faith we also must have if we are going to make it through *our* great trial during the time of trouble.

But please note, Jesus did not wait until Gethsemane to develop this type of faith. Remember, all along He said, "I do not seek My own will but the will of the Father who sent Me" (John 5:30). And, "I have come down from heaven, not to do My own will, but the will of Him who sent Me" (John 6:38). Throughout His life He practiced this same type of faith and made this same level of surrender. Notice also the following quotation from *The Ministry of Healing*.

> Christ in His life on earth made no plans for Himself. He accepted God's plans for Him, and day by day the Father unfolded His plans. So should we depend upon God, that our lives may be the simple outworking of His will. As we commit our ways to Him, He will direct our steps (p. 479).

Therefore, if we are going to make it through our great trial and keep from worshiping the beast and receiving its mark, we will need to have the same type of faith that Jesus showed throughout His life and especially in the Garden of Gethsemane. But, just like Jesus, we must develop this faith *now*. We dare not risk waiting and trying to supply this need at the last minute like the foolish virgins in the parable (Matt. 25:1-13).

Putting into practice the counsel of Proverbs 3:5, 6 can help us build the habit of exercising this type of faith. It says, "Trust in the Lord with all your heart, and lean not on your own understanding; In all your ways acknowledge Him, and He shall direct your paths." May we faithfully, moment by moment, acknowledge God in all our ways, make a complete surrender to His wisdom and His will, and let Him direct our paths.

The following quotations from Ellen White are shared here to help round out the ideas in this chapter and encourage you to make a total surrender to God's love, wisdom, and will.

> Without Christ we cannot subdue a single sin or overcome the smallest temptation (*Testimonies for the Church*, vol. 4, p. 355).

The Lord is ever setting before us, not the way we would choose, which is easier and pleasanter to us, but the true aims of life. None can neglect or defer this work but at the most fearful peril to their souls (*Maranatha*, p. 275).

Consecrate yourself to God in the morning; make this your very first work. Let your prayer be, "Take me, O Lord, as wholly Thine. I lay all my plans at Thy feet. Use me today in Thy service. Abide with me, and let all my work be wrought in Thee." This is a daily matter. Each morning consecrate yourself to God for that day. Surrender all your plans to Him, to be carried out or given up as His providence shall indicate. Thus day by day you may be giving your life into the hands of God, and thus your life will be molded more and more after the life of Christ (*Steps to Christ*, p. 70).

The third angel's message is the proclamation of the commandments of God and the faith of Jesus Christ. The commandments of God have been proclaimed, but the faith of Jesus Christ has not been proclaimed by Seventh-day Adventists as of equal importance, the law and the gospel going hand in hand (*Selected Messages*, book 3, p. 172).

Chapter 9

Let God Plan for You

We all have things we want to do. We have plans for next year, next month, tomorrow, even plans for the rest of today. As Proverbs 19:21 starts out, "There are many plans in a man's heart." But our plans don't always work out. All too often things happen that mess up our plans. So this verse goes on to contrast them with God's plans saying, "Nevertheless the Lord's counsel—that will stand." Although our plans may or may not happen, God's plans always work out! Nothing or nobody can mess up God's plans! As Proverbs 21:30 tells us, "There is no wisdom or understanding or counsel against the Lord."

In his love God also has plans for us. In Jeremiah 29:11 He tells us, "For I know the thoughts that I think toward you, says the LORD, thoughts of peace and not of evil, to give you a future and a hope." And we are probably all familiar with the verse in John 14:1-3 where Jesus promises:

> Let not your heart be troubled; you believe in God, believe also in Me. In My Father's house are many mansions; if it were not so, I would have told you. I go to prepare a place for you. And if I go and prepare a place for you, I will come again and receive you to Myself; that where I am, there you may be also.

Christ's Object Lessons provides the following comment on this verse: "Not more surely is the place prepared for us in the heavenly mansions than is the special place designated on earth where we are to work for God" (p. 327). God has a place for *us* in His plan. So, since God's plans always work out, if we are willing to fill our place in His plan, we will be carried along with His plan!

But notice the last phrase of this quotation again: there is a "special place designated on earth where we are to *work for God*." Not only does He have a place for us in His plan but He also has things planned for us to do. Unfortunately, many of us get into trouble on this point. We like the idea of God planning to give us "hope" and a "future," of Him planning a place for us in heaven, and even the assurance of success by being able to be carried through along with His plan, but we have things we want to do. The work God has for us might just take up so much of our time that we will not be able to pursue our own plans.

There is another issue closely related to this one—that God's plans may actually stand in the way of our plans. For example, how many young people have said something like, "Yes, I want Jesus to come, but there are things I want to do first, like get married and have a family." There's something we don't like about the idea of God's plans overriding our plans.

This issue goes all the way back to the tree of the knowledge of good and evil. The serpent told Eve that if she ate the fruit her "eyes [would] be opened, and [she would] be like God, knowing good and evil" (Gen. 3:5). The implication being that eating the fruit would make her wise enough to choose and plan for herself, that she wouldn't need God to tell her what to do. And ever since then the human race has tenaciously clung to the idea of making our own plans and pursuing our own agenda. Many people, like the citizens in the parable in Luke 19, have consciously or subconsciously declared, "We will not have this man to reign over us" (verse 14). Indeed, the main reason the Jewish leaders hated and killed Jesus was because He stood in the way of their agenda and the things they wanted to accomplish.

So what about us? Are we going to pursue the course of the Jewish leaders, or are we going to have faith that God's plans for us are really better than our own plans? Notice the following from *The Ministry of Healing*:

> Too many, in planning for a brilliant future, make an utter failure. Let God plan for you. As a little child, trust to the guidance of Him who will "keep the feet of His saints." 1 Samuel 2:9. God never leads His children otherwise than they would choose to be led, if they could see the end from the beginning and discern the glory of the purpose which they are fulfilling as co-workers with Him (p. 479).

Instead of planning our own agenda, we are encouraged to trust God's guidance and let Him plan for us. Note particularly the promise in the last sentence: "God never leads His children otherwise than they would choose to be led, if they could see the end from the beginning and discern the glory of the purpose which they are fulfilling as co-workers with Him." We can trust God's foresight and purpose to lead us the same way we would choose to be led if we could see things the way He sees them.

On the surface this sound good, and we may be willing to admit that we should let God plan for us. After all, we know this is the "right" answer. But let's be honest and look deeper into the issue. Is it really safe to let Him plan for us? What about the things He has put some of His people through? The classic example of this is probably Job. Look at all he went through as a result of submitting to God's plan. If Job could have seen the end from the beginning and knew all that would happen to him, would he have chosen to go through it?

At the end of the story of Job, he has ten more children and ends up with twice as much wealth as before (Job 42:10-17). But was this worth all he went through? I don't think so. As any loving parent knows, no amount of wealth would have made up for the loss of even one child—and he lost ten! And simply having more children would not have made up for ones he lost.

But let's look at the bigger picture. The "end," especially in Job's case, isn't just the way the account ends in the book that bears his name. His story has served as an encouragement and blessing to innumerable people throughout the ages, and many of them will be in the kingdom as a result of Job's testimony. If before these things happened Job could have been transported into the future and looked back and seen how many people his story would bless; if he had also understood how his experience would help to vindicate God and His dealings before the universe; if he trusted the salvation of his children to God and had faith in the resurrection; *then* I think Job would have chosen to go through all he did.

From a selfish point of view, this probably does not make any sense. Why go through all that loss and suffering just to encourage other people. And God can take care of Himself. No thank you!

But remember, Job was already a godly man before these things happened to him (see Job 1:1). By the time the account of his story begins, he would have already allowed the Holy Spirit and God's grace to change him, so he would have been driven by unselfish principles. Thus, he would have been willing to go through this experience for the sake of those who would benefit as a result.

Jesus Himself gives us another example of being willing to go through a difficult situation for the sake of those who would benefit. Hebrews 12:2 tells us, "for the joy that was set before Him endured the cross." For the sake of those who would be saved and receive eternal life, Jesus was willing to "endure the cross." He was even joyful in the anticipated result of His suffering.

Selfishness versus unselfishness is again the real issue here. Whether we choose to submit to God's plan or not will ultimately depend on whether we believe God's way of unselfishness is best, or if our own selfish way is better. May we be willing to choose God's way even though it may bring us pain and suffering.

All this becomes very practical for us living in the end-times. What if God has something similar to the cross or what Job went through planned for *us*? We may not understand how going through these things will benefit anybody. But at the time Job was going through his experience, he probably didn't see how it would be a blessing to anyone either. Therefore, like Job, we will simply have to trust God's wisdom, and in faith cling to Him.

Thus we see that to choose to stay true and endure to the end we will need a strong faith—much stronger than what we can come up with on our own. But remember, Jesus said, "Without Me you can do nothing" (John 15:5). This is one big reason we need to let God plan for us. As a part of His plan, He will train us to be unselfish, and teach us to have the kind of faith we will need to make it through to the end.

In His life on earth, Jesus gave us an example of how this works. Note the following quotation from *The Desire of Ages*:

> "The Son can do nothing of Himself, but what He seeth the Father do." [John 5:19] ... The Son of God was surrendered to the Father's will, and dependent upon His power. So utterly was Christ emptied of self that He made no plans for Himself. He accepted God's plans for Him, and day by day the Father unfolded His plans. So should we depend upon God, that our lives may be the simple outworking of His will (p. 208).

Jesus "accepted God's plans for Him" because He was "emptied of self." *Steps to Christ* adds to this by pointing out that emptying ourselves of self and submitting to God's plan is a daily matter.

> Consecrate yourself to God in the morning; make this your very first work. Let your prayer be, "Take

me, O Lord, as wholly Thine. I lay all my plans at Thy feet. Use me today in Thy service. Abide with me, and let all my work be wrought in Thee." This is a daily matter. Each morning consecrate yourself to God for that day. Surrender all your plans to Him, to be carried out or given up as His providence shall indicate. Thus day by day you may be giving your life into the hands of God, and thus your life will be molded more and more after the life of Christ (p. 70).

May we get to know God *now* so that from our own experience we will be certain that we *can* trust Him with every aspect of our lives. May we realize that in His wisdom and love He really can do a better job of planning and leading our lives than we can do for ourselves. And thus may we choose, not what we selfishly want to do, or to pursue our own plans (see Gal. 5:17), but to let God lead us and plan for us. May we be able to say along with the apostle Paul, "I am not ashamed, for I know whom I have believed and am persuaded that He is able to keep what I have committed to Him until that Day" (2 Tim. 1:12).

Ellen White offers the following council on seeking God's plans and guidance.

Many are unable to make definite plans for the future. Their life is unsettled. They cannot discern the outcome of affairs, and this often fills them with anxiety and unrest. Let us remember that the life of God's children in this world is a pilgrim life. We have not wisdom to plan our own lives. It is not for us to shape our future. "By faith Abraham, when he was called to go out into a place which he should after receive for an inheritance, obeyed; and he went out, not knowing whither he went." Hebrews 11:8.

Christ in His life on earth made no plans for Himself. He accepted God's plans for Him, and day by day the Father unfolded His plans. So should we depend upon God, that our lives may be the simple outworking of His will. As we commit our ways to Him, He will direct our steps.

Too many, in planning for a brilliant future, make an utter failure. Let God plan for you. As a little child, trust to the guidance of Him who will "keep the feet of His saints." 1 Samuel 2:9. God never leads His children otherwise than they would choose to be led, if they could see the end from the beginning and discern the glory of the purpose which they are fulfilling as co-workers with Him (*The Ministry of Healing*, pp. 478, 479).

It is natural for us to have much self-confidence and to follow our own ideas, and in so doing we separate from God ... We should be much in prayer. We need Jesus as our counselor; at every step we need him as our guide and protector. If there was more praying, more pleading with God to work for us, there would be greater dependence upon him, and faith would be strengthened to take him at his word (*Gospel Workers*, pp. 418, 419).

Chapter 10

Enmity

Romans 8:7 says, "the carnal mind is enmity against God." But what does "enmity" mean? Since we don't use this word very often, we may be tempted just to skip over it and read on. But it is an important spiritual concept we need to understand, because in a very significant way it figures into our relationship with God and our faith in Him.

The word comes up again in James 4:4, which says, "Do you not know that friendship with the world is enmity with God?" From these two verses we get the idea that enmity has to do with opposition toward God. But it's a bit more complicated than that.

The first time we find the concept of enmity in Scripture is right after Adam and Eve eat the fruit from the tree of the knowledge of good and evil. First, they realize they are naked. Then they make clothing for themselves out of leaves and hide from God when He comes into the garden (Gen. 3:7, 8). Thus one of the first results of sin is hiding from God, or to put some sort of barrier between us and Him.

And ever since, because "all have sinned," there is something in our sinful human nature that wants to keep some kind of barrier, or at least keep some distance, between ourselves and God (Rom. 3:23; see also Ps. 51:5). There doesn't necessarily have to be open hostility as the word enmity somewhat implies, we just want God to stay "over there" and leave us alone while we stay "over here" and do our own thing.

This desire to hide from God can be observed in young and old. It stems from the pride and selfishness associated with our sinful condition. We instinctively know who and what God is— the mighty all-powerful Creator (see Rom. 1:18-20). Facing Him would be humiliating. If we were to come in contact with Him, we would be forced to recognize His authority over us and our responsibility to Him. We would have to admit that we have not lived up to this responsibility. We could also no longer do what we want to do as we would have to submit to His authority (see Gal. 5:17). Our selfishness and pride just don't want to deal with any of this, so our human nature is always trying to keep God away. This is what enmity is all about.

It was this same pride and lack of humility that caused Satan to fall. Notice the following quotations from *Patriarchs and Prophets*:

> Lucifer came to indulge the desire for self-exaltation. The Scripture says, "Thine heart was lifted up because of thy beauty, thou hast corrupted thy wisdom by reason of thy brightness." Ezekiel 28:17. "Thou hast said in thine heart, ... I will exalt my throne above the stars of God.... I will be like the Most High." Isaiah 14:13, 14 (p. 35).

> Lucifer was convinced that he was in the wrong. He saw that "the Lord is righteous in all His ways, and holy in all His works" (Psalm 145:17); that the divine statutes are just, and that he ought to acknowledge them as such before all heaven. Had he done this, he might have saved himself and many angels. He had not at that time fully cast off his allegiance to God. Though he had left his position as covering cherub, yet if he had been willing to return to God, acknowledging the Creator's wisdom, and satisfied to fill the place appointed him in God's great plan, he would have been reinstated in his office. The time had come for a final decision; he must

fully yield to the divine sovereignty or place himself in open rebellion. He nearly reached the decision to return, but pride forbade him. It was too great a sacrifice for one who had been so highly honored to confess that he had been in error, that his imaginings were false, and to yield to the authority which he had been working to prove unjust (p. 39).

Let's not be like Lucifer, or we will end up like him. May we humble ourselves in the sight of the Lord and let Him lift us up (James 4:10).

When God created us, He intended for us to have a close relationship with Him. Ages ago it was observed that there is a God-shaped empty place inside each of us that only God can fill. Thus just as He came down to the garden looking for Adam and Eve after they sinned, He is constantly seeking to draw us back to Himself. "The Lord has appeared of old to me, saying: Yes, I have loved you with an everlasting love; therefore with lovingkindness I have drawn you" (Jer. 31:3). This is why Jesus came and died, so we could be brought back together with God. He said, "If I am lifted up" on the cross, I "will draw all peoples to Myself" (John 12:32). "The sinner may resist this love, may refuse to be drawn to Christ; but if he does not resist he will be drawn to Jesus" (*Steps to Christ*, p. 27). God wants to bring us back to Himself and fill our emptiness and lack of fulfillment. Jesus said, "I have come that they may have life, and that they may have it more abundantly" (John 10:10). Yet, we have all felt the same conflict inside us that Lucifer felt. One part of us wants to respond to God, another part wants to keep Him away. Let's not let our selfishness and pride keep us from connecting with Him.

Satan knows all about our enmity. Thus, he is constantly trying to take advantage of our desire to keep God at a distance, and he distracts us with literally anything that will keep us from connecting with God. A friend once pointed out that the Christian's choice isn't so much between good and evil— as we know what evil is, and we won't choose it. Our choice is between what is "good" and what is best. By getting us to choose "good" things, Satan tries to keep us from choosing the "best" thing. For example, it is quite possible to be so busy working *for* God that we don't take time to stay connected *with* Him.

Notice the following paragraph from *The Great Controversy*:

> A prayerful study of the Bible would show Protestants the real character of the papacy and would cause them to abhor and to shun it; but many are so wise in their own conceit that they feel no need of humbly seeking God that they may be led into the truth. Although priding themselves on their enlightenment, they are ignorant both of the Scriptures and of the power of God. They must have some means of quieting their consciences, and *they seek that which is least spiritual and humiliating. What they desire is a method of forgetting God which shall pass as a method of remembering Him.* The papacy is well adapted to meet the wants of all these. *It is prepared for two classes of mankind, embracing nearly the whole world—those who would be saved by their merits, and those who would be saved in their sins.* Here is the secret of its power (p. 572, emphasis added).

Our pride and enmity cause us to "seek that which is least spiritual and humiliating." It causes us to quiet our consciences with "a method of *forgetting* God which shall *pass* as a method of remembering Him." Although legalism and cheap grace appear to be opposites, they are both attempts to attain salvation without really connecting with God. Legalism tries to earn salvation apart from God, whereas cheap grace holds that since there is nothing *we* can do to earn salvation it doesn't really matter whether we live apart from God or not. Both of these theological systems allow people to continue to "hide" from God while passing as methods of "remembering Him."

The truth is, we need God, and we need a Savior. We need Him to invade our lives and change our pride and our sinful, selfish, unresponsive hearts (see Ezek. 36:26, 27). Jesus says, "*abide* in Me" like a branch that stays connected to the vine (John 15:1-6). Please don't let your enmity keep you from letting God's Spirit dwell in you. "Humble yourselves in the sight of the Lord, and *He* will lift you up" (James 4:10).

Chapter 11

Hiding or Abiding?

Hiding from God is a recurring theme throughout the Bible. As noted in the previous chapter, we first see this behavior after Adam and Eve sinned when they hid in the bushes as God came to see them in the cool of the evening (Gen. 3:8). And at the very end, we also find people hiding from God when they cry out to the mountains and rocks, "Fall on us and hide us from the face of Him who sits on the throne and from the wrath of the Lamb!" (Rev. 6:16). Throughout the history of sin, people have been trying to avoid contact with God, and Satan and human nature have come up with unnumbered schemes attempting to put some sort of barrier between us and God.

As also noted in the previous chapter, many "desire ... a method of forgetting God which shall pass as a method of remembering Him" (*The Great Controversy*, p. 572). We find this same theme in several of Jesus' parables. The people are surprised when they are rejected and cast out of the kingdom with the statement, "I do not know you." This should be a major warning to us. Notice in particular the following two examples from Matthew 7:21, 23 and 25:1-13.

> "Not everyone who says to Me, 'Lord, Lord,'
> shall enter the kingdom of heaven, but he who does
> the will of My Father in heaven. Many will say to
> Me in that day, 'Lord, Lord, have we not prophesied
> in Your name, cast out demons in Your name, and
> done many wonders in Your name?' And then I will

declare to them, 'I never knew you; depart from Me, you who practice lawlessness!'"

"Then the kingdom of heaven shall be likened to ten virgins who took their lamps and went out to meet the bridegroom. Now five of them were wise, and five were foolish. Those who were foolish took their lamps and took no oil with them, but the wise took oil in their vessels with their lamps. But while the bridegroom was delayed, they all slumbered and slept.

"And at midnight a cry was heard: 'Behold, the bridegroom is coming; go out to meet him!' Then all those virgins arose and trimmed their lamps. And the foolish said to the wise, 'Give us some of your oil, for our lamps are going out.' But the wise answered, saying, 'No, lest there should not be enough for us and you; but go rather to those who sell, and buy for yourselves.' And while they went to buy, the bridegroom came, and those who were ready went in with him to the wedding; and the door was shut.

"Afterward the other virgins came also, saying, 'Lord, Lord, open to us!' But he answered and said, 'Assuredly, I say to you, I do not know you.'"

Also pay particular attention to the following comment on this last parable from *Christ's Object Lessons*:

The class represented by the foolish virgins are not hypocrites. They have a regard for the truth, they have advocated the truth, they are attracted to those who believe the truth; but they have not yielded themselves to the Holy Spirit's working. They have not fallen upon the Rock, Christ Jesus, and permitted their old nature to be broken up. This class are represented also by the stony-ground hearers. They receive the word with readiness, but they fail of assimilating its principles. Its influence is not abiding. The Spirit works upon man's heart, according to his desire and consent implanting in him a new nature; but the class represented by the foolish virgins have been content with a superficial work. They do not know God. They have not studied His character; they have not held communion with Him; therefore they do not know how to trust, how to look and live. Their service to God degenerates into a form. "They come unto thee as the people cometh, and they sit before thee as My people, and they hear thy words, but they will not do them; for with their mouth they show much love, but their heart goeth after their covetousness." Ezekiel 33:31. The apostle Paul points out that this will be the special characteristic of those who live just before Christ's second coming. He says, "In the last days perilous times shall come: for men shall be lovers of their own selves; ... lovers of pleasures more than lovers of God; having a form of godliness, but denying the power thereof." 2 Timothy 3:1-5 (p. 411).

Did you catch that? The foolish virgins *are* virgins—just like the wise. They claim to be Christians. They "have a regard for the truth," they have lamps which are lit, and they are going out to meet the bridegroom. So where did they go wrong?

Notice what else was said about them. "The class represented by the foolish virgins have been *content with a superficial work.*" They never went deep with God. They thought a shallow Christianity was good enough. The quotation goes on to say that as a result, *"They do not know God.* They have not studied His character; *they have not held communion with Him.*" In spite of apparently being religious people, they allowed themselves to be deceived with some scheme that kept them from actually connecting with God and getting to know Him and trust Him. Therefore, "their service to God degenerates into a form"—they are just going through the motions.

Then comes the scary part, "the apostle Paul points out that *this* will be the *special characteristic* of those who live just before Christ's second coming." This is what we can expect to see all around us! And if we are honest, this is exactly what we do see all around us! In itself, this tends to deceive us as it makes it easy for us to think that shallow Christianity is normal, that this is really all there is to it. So it's not just the obvious ways of hiding from God, such as atheism and the theory of evolution that we need to avoid. We need to watch out for these more subtle deceptions, which are potentially even more dangerous.

Another one of these subtle deceptions, which was alluded to above, is not studying for ourselves. Even though we may be listening to godly preachers or reading godly authors, we still need our own personal connection with God. Keep in mind what is said in *Christ's Object Lessons*.

> Many who profess to be Christians neglect the claims of God, and yet they do not feel that in this there is any wrong. They … enjoy the services of religion. They love to hear the gospel preached, and therefore they think themselves Christians (p. 365).

Just enjoying religion and its services is not enough. Remember, the foolish virgins had lamps that were lit, and they were going out to meet the bridegroom.

Another one of these schemes is being so busy working for God that we don't take time to connect with Him. Possibly we once were connected to God—that's why we are so busy working for Him—but then we get too busy to keep up the connection and our natural enmity sneaks in. Keep in mind that our human nature wants to hide from God, and this is something we will likely have to struggle with until we are changed when Jesus comes.

Still another way we hide from God, which was pointed out in an earlier chapter, is by shutting ourselves away from nature. *Testimonies for the Church* brings this out where it says, "Those who sacrifice simplicity to fashion, and shut themselves away from the beauties of nature, cannot be spiritually minded" (vol. 2, p. 584). Unfortunately, nature isn't even a part of most people's reality anymore, so it definitely is not fashionable to connect with nature. But please notice that it did not say that we would just have a hard time being spiritual if we stayed away from nature, it said we *"cannot* be spiritually minded"—in other words, *it is impossible!* No wonder there is such a lack of spirituality in the world nowadays.

However, to be honest, there is another group that appears to connect with nature yet is still hiding from God. Although they go out into nature, which is probably better than staying indoors, for them, nature is a big playground, and they go essentially seeking another ride at the amusement park. If the "nature activity" doesn't give them a "rush," they're not really interested. In all the excitement, it's easy to avoid God without even thinking about it.

Probably subconsciously, we realize that slowing down and truly connecting with nature would also mean connecting with nature's Creator, and this would mean facing His claims on us. Please don't misunderstand me here, it is not wrong to enjoy nature; God has created an exciting world for us to live in. But we must not stop there. If we do, we are no better than the idol worshipers who worship created things rather than the Creator Himself. We need to be really honest with ourselves and ask: Where is our focus? What are we "seeking first"?

All of this goes along with the Laodicean attitude described in Revelation 3:14-22.

> "And to the angel of the church of the Laodiceans write, 'These things says the Amen, the Faithful and True Witness, the Beginning of the creation of God: "I know your works, that you are neither cold nor hot. I could wish you were cold or hot. So then, because you are lukewarm, and neither cold nor hot, I will vomit you out of My mouth. Because you say,

'I am rich, have become wealthy, and have need of nothing'—and do not know that you are wretched, miserable, poor, blind, and naked—I counsel you to buy from Me gold refined in the fire, that you may be rich; and white garments, that you may be clothed, that the shame of your nakedness may not be revealed; and anoint your eyes with eye salve, that you may see. As many as I love, I rebuke and chasten. Therefore be zealous and repent. Behold, I stand at the door and knock. If anyone hears My voice and opens the door, I will come in to him and dine with him, and he with Me. To him who overcomes I will grant to sit with Me on My throne, as I also overcame and sat down with My Father on His throne. "He who has an ear, let him hear what the Spirit says to the churches."'"

Because we enjoy being involved with religion or getting into nature, we may think that we are OK, and that being just-warm-enough-that-it-can't-be-said-that-we're-cold is good enough. However, Jesus calls this being "lukewarm," and it is nauseating to Him. This attitude of not-needing-anything, which translates into not needing to connect with God, is really just another attempt to forget God.

As alluded to in the parables mentioned earlier, hiding from God is also a deciding factor in the judgment. Notice the judgment language of the verses that immediately follow John 3:16.

For God so loved the world that He gave His only begotten Son, that whoever believes in Him should not perish but have everlasting life. For God did not send His Son into the world to condemn the world, but that the world through Him might be saved.

"He who believes in Him is not condemned; but he who does not believe is condemned already, because he has not believed in the name of the only begotten Son of God. And this is the condemnation, that the light has come into the world, and men loved darkness rather than light, because their deeds were evil. For everyone practicing evil hates the light and does not come to the light, lest his deeds should be exposed. But he who does the truth comes to the light, that his deeds may be clearly seen, that they have been done in God" (John 3:16-21).

The reason people are condemned in the judgment is because "light *has* come into the world." God has revealed Himself. However, "men loved darkness rather than light." Therefore they do "not come to the light" but hide back in the shadows because they want to do things they know God does not approve of. However, in the last verse of this passage, we find that there *are* those who do come to "the light," and it can be "clearly seen" that what they do has "been done *in* God."

Brothers and sisters, God doesn't want us to hide from Him. When Adam and Eve were back in the bushes, *He* came looking for them! His "light *has* come into the world" searching for *us*! God wants to connect with us. Jesus says:

> "Abide in Me, and I in you. As the branch cannot bear fruit of itself, unless it abides in the vine, neither can you, unless you abide in Me. I am the vine, you are the branches. He who abides in Me, and I in him, bears much fruit; for without Me you can do nothing" (John 15:4, 5).

Jesus knows we cannot make it on our own. He wants us to abide in Him and He in us so that as a result of the influence of the indwelling Holy Spirit the things we do will be "done in God." This brings us to the simple question, are we "hiding" or are we "abiding"? Brothers and sisters, let's not hide from God. Let's allow Him find us and bring us to Himself, and may our goal be to continually abide in Him.

Chapter 12

Do We Really Believe Jesus Is Coming Soon?

The Adventist Identity Crisis

Ask just about any group of Adventist Christians if they believe Jesus is coming soon and they will heartily answer, "Yes!" But let's be honest. Most of us probably say that simply because we know it is the "right answer" to the question. We've been trained that way since many of us were little children. But do we *really believe* Jesus is coming soon—within the near future?

The problem is, ever since the Millerite movement in the early 1800s, we have been saying, "Jesus is coming soon." But guess who hasn't shown up yet. When faced with this fact, many of us are embarrassed and don't really know what to say. Our grandparents have told us about people who were old, when *they* were young, that thought Jesus would come while they were still teenagers. And now, after having lived full lives, they are all dead and gone. And so, although we say we believe Jesus is coming "soon," many of us conclude that Jesus actually won't be coming back for quite a while, that we probably won't have to deal with it in our lifetime.

In his address to the North American Division teacher's

convention in Nashville in the summer of 2006, George Knight spoke of how we are in danger of losing our "apocalyptic vision." Unfortunately, I think I would have to go even farther and say that many of us have already lost the vision of the second coming happening in the near future. As a people, it seems we have slipped into "maintenance mode." Instead of planning to go to heaven soon, we are planning to be here on earth for a while, so we reason that we may as well prosper and enjoy life while we're here. Thus our thinking is absorbed with worldly things. Some of us don't even talk about the end-time prophecies anymore. Why should we if we aren't going to have to deal with these events in our lifetime? Besides, the end-times are too scary to even think about!

Although we may not admit it, even to ourselves, like the unfaithful servant in Matthew 24:48, we think in our hearts, "my Lord delays His coming," and off we go to party in the world. We overlook the fact that this very delay has been prophesied! Remember the parable of the ten virgins in Matthew 25:1-13? The bridegroom delays his coming, and this delay is a key part of the parable! Without the delay there would not have been a noticeable difference between the wise and the foolish virgins. In fact, it was the delay that separated the wise from the foolish.

The "oil" in this parable symbolizes the Holy Spirit (see Zech. 4:1-6). So, the "extra oil" must represent an "extra" portion of the Holy Spirit, which reminds us of Elisha's request for a double portion of the Spirit when Elijah was taken to heaven (see 2 Kings 2:9). Since this parable is about God's people in the end-times, it is safe to say that the delay happens to make it obvious who, like Elisha, really wants more of God in their lives and who, like the foolish virgins and the Laodiceans, think they have enough (see Rev. 3:17).

This is especially interesting in light of one of the things that came out of Operation Global Rain in the summer of 2007. People are afraid to get excited about spiritual things because they might be disappointed. But Elisha didn't want more of the

Holy Spirit just so he could be a part of some excitement or because he was afraid he might miss out on something. He wanted the extra portion of the Holy Spirit to be part of who he was. So, the question begs to be asked. Do we really want more of what God has for us? Or are we content with the amount we have and more concerned about losing time that we could have spent doing something else?

This reminds me of something we all probably did when we were children. Our parents would leave for the evening and give us a job to do before they got back. But like the children we were, we would think, "Oh, we've got *lots* of time," and off we would go to play. But then, suddenly we'd look at the clock and realize that it was already past the time our parents should have returned! Did we think, "Oh, since they haven't come back as soon as we thought they would, obviously they must not be coming back for a long time yet?" No! We would panic and frantically try to finish our job before they did show up! No wonder Jesus said, "For the sons of this world are more shrewd in their generation than the sons of light" (Luke 16:8). Even naughty children are wiser than God's people! Don't misunderstand me here; I'm not saying we should panic. But maybe we do need to re-evaluate our thinking.

So, let's go a little deeper into this issue. Why did we panic and frantically go to work? Wasn't it because we really believed our parents were coming back? And we knew what would happen when they got home if we had not finished our job! Therefore, when we think in our hearts that Jesus isn't coming for quite a while yet, doesn't it show that we must really *not* believe that He is coming soon? No wonder we have lost our "apocalyptic vision." No wonder Jesus asks, "when the Son of Man comes, will He really find faith on the earth?" (Luke 18:8).

Before His death Jesus plainly told His disciples about His betrayal, arrest, and crucifixion, and He told them to "watch and pray" (Matt. 26:41; see also Matt. 20:18, 19; 26:2, 21). But in the Garden of Gethsemane, like the ten virgins in the parable, the disciples fell asleep. If they had really believed what Jesus told them about His arrest, would they have gone to sleep? No! But because of their disbelief and their own preconceived ideas, they ignored both the prophecies and what Jesus had told them to do to prepare. And like the foolish virgins, they fell asleep when they should have been preparing for the hour of the crisis.

My brothers and sisters, wake up! We don't have enough of the oil of the Holy Spirit for what is ahead! Don't be content with a shallow Laodicean spirituality. Study the prophecies and believe what Jesus has told us. Recognize that the "delay" in His coming and the church "falling asleep" have all been foretold. These things are a part of God's plan to separate out those who truly believe from those who, in spite of what they claim, really don't believe. Which side will you be on? Remember, it is our own disbelief and preconceived ideas that cause failure and disappointment. Determine that when Jesus comes He will at least find faith in *you*.

> And do this, knowing the time, that now it is high time to awake out of sleep; for now our salvation is nearer than when we first believed. The night is far spent, the day is at hand. Therefore let us cast off the works of darkness, and let us put on the armor of light (Rom. 13:11, 12).

> For the vision is yet for an appointed time; but at the end it will speak, and it will not lie. Though it tarries, wait for it; because it will surely come, it will not tarry (Hab. 2:3).

Before it is too late to go back and get more "oil," ask God to be fill you with the Holy Spirit (see Eph. 5:18). Surrender to Him daily, and allow Him to work in you so that you may be prepared to stand in the day of God.

Chapter 13

What Does It Mean to Trust Wholly in God?

Was it OK for Noah to build the ark? Of course it was, God told him, "Make yourself an ark" (Gen. 6:14). And according to Hebrews 11:7, how did he build it? "By faith Noah, being divinely warned of things not yet seen, moved with godly fear, prepared an ark for the saving of his household." So, if it was OK for Noah to build the ark, and if he was acting "by faith" when he "prepared" it, why do many people nowadays consider it a lack of faith to prepare for the things God has warned *us* about?

This is cause for special concern as it has always been Satan's goal to twist our thinking so that we end up believing the exact opposite of the truth. This is what he did with Eve at the tree of the knowledge of good and evil, deceiving her into thinking good would result from eating the fruit (Gen. 3:4, 5). And nowadays, he has succeeded in twisting the thinking of many of us regarding what it means to trust God for our physical necessities during the time of trouble.

Satan's ultimate goal is to totally twist our thinking, which is a chief characteristic of those who commit the unpardonable sin.

For example, look at the story connected with the verses about the unpardonable sin in Matthew 12:22-32. Here, a demon-possessed man, who is also blind and mute, is brought to Jesus. Jesus casts out the demon and heals the man so he can both see and speak, which is clearly a display of the Creator's power. However, in an attempt to discredit Him, the Pharisees claim He did this by satanic power. They attribute something that was obviously God's doing to Satan. In reply, Jesus pointed out the danger of their thinking and how close it was to the unpardonable sin.

The reason this totally twisted thinking is "unpardonable" is not because it is something that God is unwilling to forgive. Although the Holy Spirit may still be extending God's grace and forgiveness to us, if our thinking has become so twisted that we think God's Spirit is something evil, we will flee from our only source of help, and thus God will no longer be able to reach us. As Isaiah said:

> Woe to those who call evil good, and good evil; who put darkness for light, and light for darkness; who put bitter for sweet and sweet for bitter! Woe to those who are wise in their own eyes, and prudent in their own sight! (Isa. 5:20, 21).

Eve should have trusted what God told her about the fruit on the tree of the knowledge of good and evil. In the same way, we need to find out and then trust what *God* has to say about things in our time. Let's be honest and humble and not rely on the way things may seem to our human reasoning. Otherwise, we may end up believing the exact opposite of the truth and doing the exact opposite of what we should be doing.

A big reason many people nowadays consider it a lack of faith to prepare for the end-times may be a misapplication of a statement by Ellen White regarding making provisions for the time of trouble, together with a misunderstanding of what it means to "trust wholly in God." Both this statement and this phrase about trusting God are found in the same paragraph on page 56 of *Early Writings*.

The first sentence of a section titled "Duty In View of the Time of Trouble" says, "The Lord has shown me repeatedly that it is contrary to the Bible to make any provision for our temporal wants in the time of trouble." Here we are apparently told *not* to prepare, that the Lord has even repeatedly shown that it is "contrary to the Bible" to do so.

So, if you want an excuse to avoid having to make any preparations, it may appear that here you have it. However, is it ever safe to build your case around just one verse from the Bible or just one sentence from the Spirit of Prophecy, especially since there are other passages that clearly indicate that some form of physical preparation is indeed appropriate? For example, Noah prepared the ark; the five wise virgins brought extra oil (Matt. 25:1-13); and a quotation from *Country Living* which states, "Again and again the Lord has instructed that our people are to take their families away from the cities, into the country, where they can raise their own provisions; for in the future the problem of buying and selling will be a very serious one" (pp. 9, 10).

In the same way that the different passages in the Bible explain themselves (see Isa. 28:10), we have been told, "The testimonies themselves will be the key that will explain the messages given, as scripture is explained by scripture" (*Selected Messages*, book 1, p. 42).

So let's study the rest of the paragraph and take a look at some other passages on this same topic.

> The Lord has shown me repeatedly that it is contrary to the Bible to make any provision for our temporal wants in the time of trouble. I saw that if the saints had food laid up by them or in the field in the time of trouble, when sword, famine, and pestilence are in the land, it would be taken from them by violent hands and strangers would reap their fields.

> Then will be the time for us to trust wholly in God, and He will sustain us. I saw that our bread and water will be sure at that time, and that we shall not lack or suffer hunger; for God is able to spread a table for us in the wilderness. If necessary He would send ravens to feed us, as He did to feed Elijah, or rain manna from heaven, as He did for the Israelites (*Early Writings,* p. 56).

Notice that the main subject of this paragraph is food. This is interesting; because in the dictionary, we find essentially two sets of definitions for the word "provisions." The first refers to *all* the things we need. The second refers primarily to things that get used up as we use them, particularly food. For example, according to the second set of definitions, "provisions" would be water, but not necessarily a bottle that we might carry the water in; toilet paper, but not necessarily the toilet or sewer system; or food, but not necessarily the stove and utensils to cook it with. On the other hand, the first set of definitions would include all of these things.

Since the quotation states that "it is contrary to the Bible to make *any* provision for our temporal wants," it might seem that we should go with the first set of definitions. However, looking at the paragraph as a whole, we find that its main subject is simply food, which would actually best fit with the second set of definitions. This is also supported by looking at other places where the author uses the word "provisions," such as the *Country Living* quotation mentioned earlier about God's people moving to the country where they "can raise their own provisions." Here again we find that food is also primarily what she has in mind.

Let's look at another quotation with very similar wording as the passage from *Early Writings* that is found in the book *Maranatha.*

> The Lord has shown me in vision, repeatedly, that it is contrary to the Bible to make any provision for our temporal wants in the time of trouble. I saw that if the saints have food laid up by them, or in the fields,

in the time of trouble when sword, famine, and pestilence are in the land, it will be taken from them by violent hands, and strangers would reap their fields. Then will be the time for us to trust wholly in God, and He will sustain us. I saw that our bread and water would be sure at that time, and we should not lack, or suffer hunger. The Lord has shown me that some of His children would fear when they see the price of food rising, and they would buy food and lay it by for the time of trouble. Then in a time of need, I saw them go to their food and look at it, and it had bred worms, and was full of living creatures, and not fit for use (p. 181).

This paragraph is not just about food, it is about stocking up food for the time of trouble. This is significant because the first thing most people, Christians or non-Christians, think of when faced with "The-End-Of-Life-As-We-Know-It" scenarios is to stock up on supplies! Since the first sentence in a paragraph is frequently a topic sentence, if we understand the phrase, "to make provisions," to mean essentially the same as "stocking up supplies," particularly food, a lot of pieces fit into place.

Rather than these statements being sweeping prohibitions against *any* physical preparations for the time of trouble, as some would have us believe, the obvious message of both of these quotations, when taken as a whole, is that God's people should not try to stock up enough food or water or toilet paper for that matter to last until Jesus comes.

But it is even more important that we recognize the real issue in these paragraphs. The reason we are told not to "make any provision for our temporal wants in the time of trouble" is because "then will be the time for us to trust wholly in God." The real issue here is not so much provisions as it is trusting wholly in God.

Human reasoning may have us believe that trusting wholly in God means doing absolutely *nothing* on our part because *anything* we might do would take away from it being *wholly* God's doing. This apparently goes along with the interpretation of these quotations to mean that we should not do anything to prepare for the time of trouble. And from the standpoint of human reasoning this all appears to make sense.

However, Proverbs 3:5 states, "Trust in the Lord with all your heart, and lean not on your own understanding." Isaiah 55:8-9 also tells us, "'For My thoughts are not your thoughts, nor are your ways My ways,' says the Lord. 'For as the heavens are higher than the earth, so are My ways higher than your ways, and My thoughts than your thoughts.'" And Proverbs 14:12 says, "There is a way that seems right to a man, but its end is the way of death." Can we trust our human reasoning or trust what might seem right to us? Absolutely not! For example, how many times, after things didn't turn out so well, have we shrugged our shoulders and thought something like, "Well, it seemed like a good thing to do at the time?"

As noted earlier, Satan's goal is to totally twist our thinking. He is able to do this only as we "lean on our own understanding," for when we are relying on God and His wisdom, he does not have power over us. Therefore, it is important that we don't trust the way things might seem to us. Instead, we need to find out what God has to say and build our thinking around what He has said regarding what it means to trust wholly in Him.

Noah gives us an excellent example on this subject. Notice what Ellen White wrote regarding Noah's actions.

> Noah did not hesitate to obey God. He urged no excuse, that the labor of building that ark was great and expensive. He believed God, and invested in the ark all that he possessed (*The Signs of the Times*, February 27, 1879).

> All that man could do was done to render the work perfect, yet the ark could not of itself have withstood

the storm which was to come upon the earth. God alone could preserve His servants upon the tempestuous waters (*Patriarchs and Prophets*, p. 95).

Preparing the ark was not an easy task, neither was it convenient or inexpensive. Noah spent a lot of his time, energy, and all of his resources on the project. The workmanship on the ark was even perfect! Yet in spite of doing all that he did, "God alone could preserve His servants upon the tempestuous waters." Even though Noah made extensive preparations, he was still trusting wholly in God alone.

According to human reasoning, this doesn't make sense either. Why should Noah have to spend "all that he possessed"? Why would he have to labor diligently for 120 years if it was "God alone" who could get him through the flood? Suppose, based on the way this "seems" to human reasoning, Noah had said something like, "I just don't understand why I should have to spend all my time, energy, and resources preparing an ark. God has promised to take care of us, so when the time comes, I'll just trust wholly in Him. Besides, there are all these people who need to hear God's message, and so many hurting people that need to be ministered to (see Gen. 6:11). I just don't have time to spend preparing an ark." If for whatever reason Noah had not built the ark, what would have happened to him? He would have no doubt died in the flood.

Jesus said, "As the days of Noah were, so also will the coming of the Son of Man be" (Matt. 24:37). And 1 Corinthians 10:11 says, "All these things happened to them as examples, and they were written for our admonition, upon whom the ends of the ages have come." Among other things, God had Noah prepare the ark as an example for us! Apparently, the human reasoning that tells us, "If we do anything, then it is not wholly God's doing," is just that, human reasoning, and not the ways or thoughts of God.

Analyzing Noah's example, we find several significant points. First, it is not necessary to do nothing or have nothing to be trusting

Faith for These End-Times

in "God alone." Second, like Noah, we may have to spend a lot of our time, energy, and resources preparing for the things God has warned us about—and these preparations do not necessarily detract from trusting wholly in God. However, the third point is that, it is very important that whatever we do be done *by faith*—as there were many things Noah could have done in preparation for the flood that would not have been "by faith," none of which would have actually helped him make it through the crisis.

Let us look at another example that illustrates these same points, for "in a multitude of counselors there is safety" (Prov. 24:6). The following is a description of the experience of the Israelites at the Red Sea from *Patriarchs and Prophets*.

> God in His providence brought the Hebrews into the mountain fastnesses before the sea, that He might manifest His power in their deliverance and signally humble the pride of their oppressors. He might have saved them in any other way, but He chose this method in order to test their faith and strengthen their trust in Him. The people were weary and terrified, yet if they had held back when Moses bade them advance, God would never have opened the path for them. It was "by faith" that "they passed through the Red Sea as by dry land." Hebrews 11:29. In marching down to the very water, they showed that they believed the word of God as spoken by Moses. They did all that was in their power to do, and then the Mighty One of Israel divided the sea to make a path for their feet.
>
> The great lesson here taught is for all time. Often the Christian life is beset by dangers, and duty seems hard to perform. The imagination pictures impending ruin before and bondage or death behind. Yet the voice of God speaks clearly, "Go forward." We should obey this command, even though our eyes cannot penetrate the darkness, and

we feel the cold waves about our feet. The obstacles that hinder our progress will never disappear before a halting, doubting spirit. Those who defer obedience till every shadow of uncertainty disappears and there remains no risk of failure or defeat, will never obey at all. Unbelief whispers, "Let us wait till the obstructions are removed, and we can see our way clearly;" but faith courageously urges an advance, hoping all things, believing all things (p. 290).

Notice that God "might have saved them in any other way, but He chose this method in order to *test their faith* and *strengthen their trust* in Him." By this experience He was teaching the Israelites to "trust wholly in God." Did you also note the last sentence of the first paragraph? "They did *all that was in their power to do*, and *then* the Mighty One of Israel divided the sea to make a path for their feet." So trusting wholly in God includes doing all that is in our power to do! If the Israelites had relied on their own understanding and thought, "If we do anything then it won't be wholly God's doing," and expected God to take care of them while they did nothing, "God would never have opened the path for them." Again, it was very important for them to act "by faith" as they "did all that was in their power to do," since there were certainly other things they could have done that would not have been "by faith." But because they obeyed the command to "go forward," trusting wholly in God, He made a way of escape for them.

Notice also that "the great lesson here taught is for *all time*." This same lesson applies now and will continue to apply to our experience throughout the time of trouble. In other words, the "rules" don't change after the close of probation during the second part of the time of trouble as some have suggested. They have thought that we have been told to do specific things to prepare for the first part of the time of trouble, such as having a place in the country where we can raise our own provisions. But, from the way the author uses the term the time of trouble in the quotations from *Early Writings* and *Maranatha* (at this point in her experience) and the wilderness context of these quotations, it is evident that they refer primarily to the second part of the time of trouble. Therefore, since these quotations tell us not to "make any provision for our temporal wants" there must be a change in God's policy at the close of probation. Although we have an active part to play up until then, during the second part of the time of trouble we are to do essentially nothing and just "trust wholly in God." But this quotation from *Patriarchs and Prophets* shows that this is not the case. "Jesus Christ *is* the same yesterday, today, and forever." (Heb. 13:8).

Let's look at another example, this time from the New Testament. It is found in Matthew 6:26. This verse is quoted in the commentary below from *Steps to Christ*.

> In His Sermon on the Mount, Christ taught His disciples precious lessons in regard to the necessity of trusting in God. These lessons were designed to encourage the children of God through all ages, and they have come down to our time full of instruction and comfort. The Saviour pointed His followers to the birds of the air as they warbled their carols of praise, unencumbered with thoughts of care, for 'they sow not, neither do they reap.' And yet the great Father provides for their needs. The Saviour asks, 'Are ye not much better than they?' Matthew 6:26. The great Provider for man and beast opens His hand and supplies all His creatures. The birds of the air are not beneath His notice. He does not drop the food into their bills, but He makes provision for their needs. They must gather the grains He has scattered for them. They must prepare the material for their little nests. They must feed their young. They go forth singing to their labor, for 'your heavenly Father feedeth them.' And 'are ye not much better than they?' Are not you, as intelligent,

spiritual worshipers, of more value than the birds of the air? Will not the Author of our being, the Preserver of our life, the One who formed us in His own divine image, provide for our necessities if we but trust in Him?

Did you notice where it said "Christ taught His disciples *precious lessons* in regard to *the necessity of trusting in God*"? Note that it also said that "these lessons were designed to encourage the children of God through all ages, and they have come down to our time full of instruction and comfort." The lessons found here about the "necessity of trusting in God" are also for us during the end-times.

To teach these lessons, Jesus points us to the birds and tells us how the Father provides for them. But "He does not drop the food into their bills." The human reasoning mentioned earlier makes it seem that during the final part of the time of trouble God will essentially do just that. But here we are told that this is *not* God's way of doing things, even in the end-times.

There is a similar passage found in the *Review and Herald*, September 18, 1888, that adds a key thought to this discussion. It says, "He does not drop the food into their bills, but he makes provision for their needs. They must *exert themselves* to gather the grains he has scattered for them" (emphasis added).

Maybe Laodicean laziness is the real problem here! We like the idea of not having to exert ourselves. Our selfish desire for comfort and convenience, which has been heavily reinforced by our modern culture, would like to have us believe that, without any effort on our part, we can just "trust wholly in God" and our stomachs will be filled and we will be at ease even in the wilderness! After all, aren't we promised that "He would send ravens to feed us, as He did to feed Elijah, or rain manna from heaven, as He did for the Israelites" (*Early Writings*, p. 56). Doesn't this promise imply that we don't need to worry about preparing, that all the exertion we will probably have to do is just reach up and take the food as the ravens hold it out to us?

If we are tempted to think this, let us be careful to not over-look the first two words of that sentence about the ravens and manna. It says, *"If necessary* He would send ravens to feed us, as He did to feed Elijah, or rain manna from heaven, as He did for the Israelites." Does "if necessary" indicate that the ravens and manna are God's main plan for providing for us? Or are the ra-vens and manna His back-up plan? Let's be honest; "if necessary" is back-up plan language!

So, if the ravens and manna are His back-up plan, what is His main plan? To find out, we need to look back at the phrase just before this sentence. It states, "God is able to spread a table for us in the wilderness." To fill out the meaning of this phrase, we need to put it together with a similar quotation from *The Ministry of Healing*, which states that "The mountains and hills are chang-ing; the earth is waxing old like a garment; but the blessing of God, which spreads for His people a table in the wilderness, will never cease" (p. 200). By saying that God's blessings, which "spreads ... a table in the wilderness, will never cease," it means these blessings will always be there in the same way they have always been there. In other words, the same blessings that have "spread ... a table in the wilderness" for God's children, the na-tive peoples who have lived off the land for thousands of years, are still there and will still be there for us when we flee to the wilderness.

Although this may be a comforting promise, we need to think about how the native peoples obtained God's blessings. They had to do the same thing as the birds. They had to exert themselves and go out and gather the things God provided for them. Therefore, God's main plan during the second part of the time of trouble is that we will exert ourselves to gather and craft the things we need from the natural resources He has provided for us in the wilder-ness in the same way that the birds and the native peoples have obtained these blessings. But if for some reason these things are not available, such as the upheavals of nature during the seven last plagues, we have the promise that "if necessary" He will send the ravens or rain manna.

As we understand the principle of doing all that is in our power while trusting wholly in God, we start finding it throughout Scripture. The only place I know where God told the people, "Stand still and see the salvation of the Lord," is in 2 Chronicles 20:17. Apparently they didn't have to exert themselves except to stand there and watch God act. However, if we look at the larger picture, we find that for a couple of generations the people had already been doing all that was in their power to prepare for such an invasion (see 2 Chron. 14-17). Thus they were already as prepared for the crisis as they could be.

Yet, like Noah, in spite of all they had done, they realized that their preparations were not enough. They still needed to rely on God alone. And as they cried out to God for deliverance, He saved them from their enemies (see 2 Chron. 20:3-30).

Many have interpreted the quote in *Early Writings* to say that we should not do anything to prepare for the time of trouble. However, if we are honest, based on the wording of this very same paragraph, we recognize that we will need a certain amount of knowledge, skills, and some basic tools to be able to make use of the things God has provided for us in nature. This will be true both for when we are living in the country raising our own provisions during the first part of the time of trouble, and for when we flee to the wilderness during the final part of the time of trouble.

A big part of our problem is in where most of us obtain our food on a day-to-day basis. If you ask a child where food comes from, he or she will probably answer something like, "from the store." Unfortunately, this has been the case for several generations now, which is helping to set us up for the mark of the beast. We are not used to getting our food (or other necessities) directly from nature. Therefore, most of us don't have the knowledge, skills, or basic tools for this type of lifestyle.

When faced with "every earthly support" being "cut off" (*The Desire of Ages*, p. 121), most people naturally think of stocking up, since that is all we know how to do. However, the quotations from *Early Writings* and *Maranatha* clearly state that we should not do this. Instead, these quotations and the other counsel we have been given regarding the time of trouble point to a time when we will be getting our necessities directly from nature, trusting the God of nature to provide for us. It appears that as a part of our final training for heaven and the new earth, God wants us to get used to depending on Him rather than "the store" for the things we need, since this is what we will be doing for the rest of eternity.

So, if we are wise, we will prepare for both our country and wilderness living experiences. We will acquire as much of the knowledge, skills, and basic tools for getting our necessities directly from nature as we can. It would also be a very good idea to practice country living and wilderness survival as much as possible, so we will know from our own experience that we can indeed trust God to provide for us directly from nature.

If we don't prepare, where will that leave us? Suppose, for example, that when we flee to the wilderness God leads us to a cave that is surrounded by many oak trees. Their nutritious acorns are falling all around us. God has indeed "spread a table for us in the wilderness." We gather some up and try to eat them, but the unprocessed acorns are very bitter! Eaten in quantity they could make us quite sick. If we have not learned the simple process of leaching out the tannic acid to render acorns edible, would it be God's fault or our own fault if we go hungry?

Acquiring these skills, knowledge, tools, and experience in preparation will not necessarily detract from trusting wholly in God. Like Noah and the Israelites, we should know that even though we do all that is in our power to do, it will still not be enough. As we raise our own provisions during the first part of the time of trouble, we will still need to trust that God will give us agricultural wisdom and cause our plants to grow and provide us with a good harvest. During the second part of the time of trouble, as we wander in the wilderness searching for our necessities, we will claim the promises, "Seek, and you will find," and "Bread shall be given him, his waters shall be sure," trusting that God will bring us to the things we need (Matt. 7:7; Isa. 33:16).

Because faith and works go together (James 2:17, 18), God cannot bless inactivity. Can we expect God to open the path for us if we don't do all that is in our power to do, even in our preparations?

This brings us to the question, "How can we know whether what we are doing to prepare is being done in faith or not?" A simple answer is found in Proverbs 3:5, 6: "Trust in the Lord with *all* your heart." "Trust in the Lord"—trust wholly in God, especially trust in His way of thinking and doing. "And lean not on your own understanding"—don't just do what seems right to human reasoning. "In all your ways acknowledge Him"—here is where it gets practical. Check in with Him before you do anything to be sure you are thinking and acting according to His ways and thoughts. Ask Him, "What do You want me to do now?" And, "How do I do this Your way?" Doing this will require spending some serious time in God's Word, searching out how God thinks about things and how He does things. To be acting "by faith" we need to be sure we are following God's instructions and doing things His way. "And He shall direct your paths"—if we acknowledge Him in all our ways, He will direct our paths and work things out for us. Like Noah, He will preserve us "upon the tempestuous waters."

We have been told, "While Noah was giving his warning message to the world, his works testified of his sincerity. It was thus that his faith was perfected and made evident. He gave the world an example of believing just what God says.… Every blow struck upon the ark was a witness to the people" (*Patriarchs and Prophets*, p. 95). Therefore, rather than showing a lack of faith, our preparations, like Noah's, will be a demonstration of our faith.

Chapter 14

For by Grace You Have Been Saved Through Faith

Grace has typically been defined as "God's unmerited favor." But this definition has essentially the same meaning as mercy. It is true that we don't deserve God's favor or mercy, but as one reads through the Bible, especially the New Testament, it seems that when the writers used the word grace, they had more in mind than just God feeling favorable and being merciful toward us.

As an example, let's look at James 4:1-6. As we read through this passage, notice the progression as James first describes a problem, then the cause of the problem, and finally, God's solution for the problem:

> Where do wars and fights come from among you? Do they not come from your desires for pleasure that war in you members? You lust and do not have. You murder and covet and cannot obtain. You fight and war. Yet you do not have because you do not ask. You ask and do not receive, because you ask amiss, that you may spend it on you pleasures. Adulterers and adulteresses! Do you not know that friendship with the

world is enmity with God? Whoever therefore wants to be a friend of the world makes himself an enemy of God. Or do you think that the Scripture says in vain, "The Spirit who dwells in us yearns jealously"? But He gives more grace. Therefore He says: "God resists the proud, but gives grace to the humble."

What is the problem that is described here? "Fights," or as some versions say, "quarrels … among you." And what is the cause of these conflicts? Our selfish "desires for pleasure." The middle part of this passage talks about how these conflicts affect both relationships among ourselves and with God. Then in the last two sentences James gives God's solution: "He gives more *grace*." More than just mercy, or feeling favorable toward us, grace is God's solution to the conflicts caused by our sinful desires.

Remember also that God is interested in permanent solutions. His goal is a universe full of peace and harmony for the rest of eternity. So He isn't going to just patch things up, or treat symptoms, or make the trouble caused by our selfish desires just go away. His solution is to go to the root, or cause, of the problem and fix it. Only by getting rid of the cause can there be any assurance that the problem will not return to make trouble again.

Since grace is God's solution to the conflicts caused by our sinful desires, in order to truly fix the problem, it must therefore, be able to get rid of these selfish desires. Hence, grace must be able to change us so that we don't even want sinful things anymore! This is much more than just God being merciful and feeling favorable toward us.

But putting this together with the last part of Romans 7, we find that even changing our sinful desires isn't enough. Notice what Paul says in the last part of verses 18 and 19. "For to will is present with me, but how to perform what is good I do not find. For the good that I will [or want] to do, I do not do; but the evil I will not to do, that I practice." Here Paul is describing the condition of a person who wants to do the right thing, whose desires are being changed. But he points out that this by itself isn't enough. Even though we may want to do the right thing, we still aren't able to do it on our own. Thus to truly fix the problem, grace must not stop with just changing our sinful desires. Grace must also enable us to do right. So to put this all together, we find that grace is both the *desire* and the *power* to do what is right.

There is no place for fights and quarrels in God's kingdom of peace and harmony. And Jesus' death on the cross gives us abundant evidence that God wants us to be a part of His kingdom. But if we are to be a part of His kingdom, we must not only *want* to do right, we must actually be able to *do* it. Therefore, it is because of His mercy and because of His feelings of favorableness toward us that God gives us His grace—both the desire and the power to do what is right. No wonder so many of the New Testament books begin, or end, with phrases such as "grace be unto you." May our faith make us willing to give up the selfish things we desire and allow God to change and empower us by His grace.

James goes on to say, "God resists the proud, but gives grace to the humble" (James 4:6). Therefore, "Humble yourselves in the sight of the Lord, and He will lift you up" (verse 10).

Ellen White offers the following inspiration in *Testimonies for the Church* regarding God's grace and the part we play in receiving it:

> Without the grace of God, men love to do evil. They walk in darkness, and do not possess the power of self-control. They give loose rein to their passions and appetites until all the finer feelings are lost and only the animal passions are manifested. Such men need to feel a higher, controlling power, which will constrain them to obey (vol. 1, p. 362).

Chapter 15

Righteousness by Faith

A book on faith would not be complete without a chapter on righteousness by faith. This topic has been saved toward the last because, hopefully, a better understanding of faith will make this concept clearer. Perhaps one reason we have struggled with understanding righteousness by faith is a lack of a good working definition, as opposed to theoretical definitions, for both "righteousness" and "faith." To begin with, we will focus on righteousness and then consider a collective definition for faith. Finally, we will put the two together and look at a story in Scripture that illustrates how it works.

Righteousness is fairly easy to define, although the concept may not be as easy to grasp. Rather than being some ethereal spiritual quality, righteousness is simply doing the right thing. "Righteousness is right doing" (*Christ's Object Lessons*, p. 312). God is righteous (in the ethereal spiritual quality sense) because, in His infinite wisdom and love, He *always* does the "right" thing. Only the Creator God knows what is best for each one of His creatures throughout the entire universe. And because of His infinite love, He not only knows but always does what is best for everyone and everything concerned.

On the other hand, we have trouble doing the right thing. If we are honest, we have to admit that our selfish human nature is rarely inclined to even be concerned with what is best for ourselves or anyone else—we simply want to do whatever we desire. For example, how often do we eat or drink something we know isn't good for us? But even when we *are* concerned about what is best, what we might think is right usually is not, simply because of our limited vision. The truth of Proverbs 14:12 is obvious, "There is a way that seems right to a man, but its end is the way of death."

We would be wise therefore to follow the counsel given in Proverbs 3:5, 6: "Trust in the Lord with all your heart, and lean not on your own understanding; in all your ways acknowledge Him, and He shall direct your paths." Although this may seem simplistic, if we would humbly recognize the inadequacies of our own understanding and, rather than leaning on it, trust and follow God's wisdom and instructions, we would do right things.

Defining faith is a little more complex. To summarize the other chapters in this book, faith believes that God's way of unselfish love is better than our own selfish way (see Isa. 55:8, 9; 1 John 4:7, 8; John 15:1-8; Heb. 11:13-16). But faith does not just believe God's way is better, it chooses God's way (see James 2:19, 23; Heb. 11:6). Faith also recognizes that even though we may choose God's way, on our own we are powerless to actually do what is loving and unselfish (see Rom. 7:15, 18, 19; John 15:5). Therefore, faith leads us to surrender to the indwelling Spirit of God (see John 14:16, 17; Acts 1:8; Ezek. 36:26, 27) and trust God's promises to complete the work He has begun in us to sanctify us and keep us for His kingdom (see Phil. 1:6; 1 Thess. 5:23, 24; Jude 24).

Righteousness by faith, therefore, is doing the right thing because of our faith in God. Thus, rather than relying on the way things might seem to us, we choose to trust His wisdom regarding what is best and right. Humbly, we recognize our own inability to do what is right, so we rely on His power working in us and through us to produce right actions. As the apostle Paul declared in Romans 1:16, 17, "I am not ashamed of the gospel of Christ, for it is the *power of God* to salvation for everyone who believes. For in it [the gospel] the *righteousness of God* is revealed … as it is written, 'The just shall live by faith.'"

When we focus on abiding in Christ by faith and surrendering to the Holy Spirit's working, we can claim the following promises: "Humble yourself in the sight of the Lord, and *He* will lift you up" (James 4:10). "You shall receive power when the Holy Spirit has come upon you" (Acts 1:8). "I will give you a new heart and put a new spirit within you; I will take the heart of stone out of your flesh and give you a heart of flesh. I will put My Spirit within you and cause you to walk in My statutes, and you will keep My judgments and do them" (Ezek. 36:26, 27). "Now may the God of peace Himself sanctify you completely; and may your whole spirit, soul, and body be preserved blameless at the coming of our Lord Jesus Christ" (1 Thess. 5:23). In this way, "the righteous require-ment of the law might be fulfilled in us who do not walk according to the flesh but according to the Spirit" (Rom. 8:4).

Righteousness by faith relies on God's wisdom to reveal what is right and on the power of the indwelling Holy Spirit to enable us to actually do the right thing. Thus, as we abide in Jesus and are filled with, and controlled by, the Holy Spirit, we will be righ-teous. This is not to say we will never sin again, as we will always be fully capable of choosing to step away from faith. Thus, in order to always do what is right, we need to develop the habit of always choosing to abide or stay in Jesus.

The experience of the disciples on the night Jesus was ar-rested gives us an excellent scriptural example of how this works. Although they had already been with Jesus for several years, they still had not learned an important lesson, that the kingdom of God is all about loving, unselfish service. Thus, on the way to the upper room, they were arguing about who was the greatest. Now, Jesus was obviously the greatest, so their debate was actually about who would be *second* greatest. The "triumphal entry" had only add-ed to their desire for an important position in the kingdom that they expected Jesus to set up soon. Like a bunch of little children crying, "Me first!" they continued to argue even during the Last Supper (Luke 22:24)!

Then Jesus washes their feet. The One who was obviously the greatest did the job of the lowest! The job none of them would have thought of doing, especially considering their current debate. As Jesus washed their feet, they were convicted of their pride, self-importance, selfishness, and unworthiness, and the Holy Spirit was able to soften their hearts (John 13:6-8). Then, as Jesus told them why He washed their feet, they realized in a new way that His kingdom is really all about unselfish service and not at all about being the greatest or the most important. So, except for Judas, who still had his own agenda, they all re-surrendered themselves to God.

Because they had responded and surrendered to the moving of the Holy Spirit, allowing His grace to change their hearts, Jesus was able to say to them, "You are clean, but not all of you" (John 13:10). Except for Judas, they were "clean," that is, without sin. Rather than seeking their own selfish interests, at that point they had put their faith in Jesus, and thus they were declared righteous. A little later after Judas left the group (John 13:30), and they are on their way to the Garden of Gethsemane, Jesus repeated His statement so there could be no mistake. He told them again, "You are already clean because of the word which I have spoken to you" (John 15:3).

From our way of thinking, this is almost unbelievable. Jesus knew they had been selfishly arguing just a short while before. He also knew they would leave and betray Him in just a few short hours (see Mark 14:27). But because at this point in time they were all, by faith, surrendered to God, He was able to say they were "clean," without sin, "righteous."

Fortunately for all of us, Jesus doesn't stop there. In His very next sentence, He gives the secret of how to stay righteous and live without sinning. He says, "Abide in Me," or as some translations put it, "remain" or "stay in Me" (John 15:4). Jesus knows our weakness and inability. He knows that our only hope is to continually remain in Him, constantly relying on His wisdom and power.

The following diagram may help to explain how this works. The top line represents abiding by faith in Jesus. The bottom line represents being out of Jesus and, therefore, in sin. Time progresses from left to right. Spiritually, we are either in one place or the other; there is no space in between for, "No one can serve two masters" (Matt. 6:24). Due to our sinful human nature, we all start out "in sin." But in time the Holy Spirit gets through to us, and we come to Jesus. However, because of our previous habits and the alluring power of sin, we don't stay in Him very long, and the next thing we know, we've slipped back into sin. Then we respond once again to the Holy Spirits influence and return to Jesus. Yet Satan distracts us, and we fall into sin again. And so, as life goes on, we go back and forth. However, as we think about where we really want to be and keep reconsecrating ourselves to Jesus, allowing the Holy Spirit to work with us, we will spend less and less time in sin, and more and more time in Jesus.

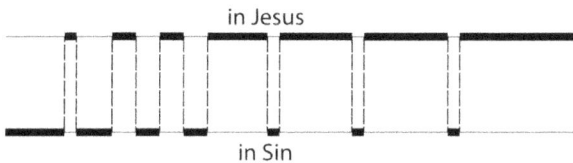

in Jesus

in Sin

To put this together with the story of Jesus' disciples, when they were arguing about who was the greatest, they were in sin. After they responded to Jesus as He washed their feet, they were in Jesus. But then, as they forsook Him and fled at His arrest, they again slipped back into sin.

As noted earlier, although we may in fact not be sinning when we are in Jesus, by our conscious or unconscious choice, we will always be fully capable of slipping back into sin. If we are honest, we will recognize how easily and quickly this can happen, and this knowledge should give us a strong sense of our weakness and cause us to hold on all the tighter to our only Source of strength. Thus we will never feel that we are righteous or without sin. Instead, a true understanding will cause us to feel our inadequacy and our complete need of continually being kept by God's power.

Thus, as by faith we continue to abide in Jesus, the day can come when we slip into sin for the last time. It is doubtful that we will recognize when this happens because we will only sense our weakness and complete dependence on His keeping power. But at that point, it would be possible for Jesus to say about us, "he who is righteous, let him be righteous still," probation could close for us as an individual, and we would be safe to take to heaven (Rev. 22:11).

In writing this it is my prayer that we will develop the habit of continually choosing by faith to surrender to the indwelling Holy Spirit that we may remain/stay/abide in Jesus and as a result do what is right.

As we close out this chapter on righteousness by faith, following are some quotes from Ellen White on this important subject.

> No outward observances can take the place of simple faith and entire renunciation of self. But no man can empty himself of self. We can only consent for Christ to accomplish the work. Then the language of the soul will be, Lord, take my heart; for I cannot give it. It is Thy property. Keep it pure, for I cannot keep it for Thee. Save me in spite of myself, my weak, unchristlike self. Mold me, fashion me, raise me into a pure and holy atmosphere, where the rich current of Thy love can flow through my soul (*Christ's Object Lessons*, p. 159).

> Consecrate yourself to God in the morning; make this your very first work. Let your prayer be, "Take me, O Lord, as wholly Thine. I lay all my plans at Thy feet. Use me today in Thy service. Abide with

me, and let all my work be wrought in Thee." This is a daily matter. Each morning consecrate yourself to God for that day. Surrender all your plans to Him, to be carried out or given up as His providence shall indicate. Thus day by day you may be giving your life into the hands of God, and thus your life will be molded more and more after the life of Christ (*Steps to Christ*, p. 70).

Do not disappoint Him who so loved you that He gave His own life to cancel your sins. He says, "Without Me ye can do nothing." John 15:5. Remember this. If you have made mistakes, you certainly gain a victory if you see these mistakes and regard them as beacons of warning. Thus you turn defeat into victory, disappointing the enemy and honoring your Redeemer (*Christ's Object Lessons*, p. 332).

Those who are in connection with God are channels for the power of the Holy Spirit. If one who daily communes with God errs from the path, if he turns a moment from looking steadfastly unto Jesus, it is not because he sins wilfully; for when he sees his mistake, he turns again, and fastens his eyes upon Jesus, and the fact that he has erred, does not make him less dear to the heart of God. He knows that he has communion with the Saviour; and when reproved for his mistake in some matter of judgment, he does not walk sullenly, and complain of God, but turns the mistake into a victory. He learns a lesson from the words of the Master, and takes heed that he be not again deceived (*Review and Herald*, May 12, 1896).

The perils of the last days are upon us. *Satan takes the control of every mind that is not decidedly under the control of the Spirit of God* (*Testimonies to Ministers*, p. 79).

[Satan] ... is constantly seeking to deceive the followers of Christ with his fatal sophistry that it is impossible for them to overcome. But Jesus pleads in their behalf His wounded hands, His bruised body; and He declares to all who would follow Him: "My grace is sufficient for thee." 2 Corinthians 12:9. "Take My yoke upon you, and learn of Me; for I am meek and lowly in heart: and ye shall find rest unto your souls. For My yoke is easy, and My burden is light." Matthew 11:29, 30. Let none, then, regard their defects as incurable. God will give faith and grace to overcome them (*The Great Controversy*, p. 489).

Satan represents God's law of love as a law of selfishness. He declares that it is impossible for us to obey its precepts. The fall of our first parents, with all the woe that has resulted, he charges upon the Creator, leading men to look upon God as the author of sin, and suffering, and death. Jesus was to unveil this deception. As one of us He was to give an example of obedience. For this He took upon Himself our nature, and passed through our experiences. "In all things it behooved Him to be made like unto His brethren." Hebrews 2:17. If we had to bear anything which Jesus did not endure, then upon this point Satan would represent the power of God as insufficient for us. Therefore Jesus was "in all points tempted like as we are." Hebrews 4:15. He endured every trial to which we are subject. And He exercised in His own behalf no power that is not freely offered to us. As man, He met temptation, and overcame in the strength given Him from God. He says, "I delight to do Thy will, O My God: yea, Thy law is within My heart." Psalm 40:8. As He went about doing good, and healing all who were afflicted by Satan, He made plain to men the character of

God's law and the nature of His service. His life testifies that it is possible for us also to obey the law of God (*The Desire of Ages*, p. 24).

Several have written to me, inquiring if the message of justification by faith is the third angel's message, and I have answered, "It is the third angel's message in verity" (*Evangelism*, p. 190).

What is justification by faith? It is the work of God in laying the glory of man in the dust, and doing for man that which it is not in his power to do for himself (*Testimonies to Ministers and Gospel Workers,* p. 456).

No matter who you are or what your life has been, you can be saved only in God's appointed way. You must repent; you must fall helpless on the Rock, Christ Jesus. You must feel your need of a physician and of the one only remedy for sin, the blood of Christ. This remedy can be secured only by repentance toward God and faith toward our Lord Jesus Christ. Here the work is yet to be begun by many who profess to be Christians and even to be ministers of Christ. Like the Pharisees of old many of you feel no need of a Saviour. You are self-sufficient, self-exalted. Said Christ: "I came not to call the righteous, but sinners to repentance." The blood of Christ will avail for none but those who feel their need of its cleansing power (*Testimonies for the Church,* vol. 5, pp. 218, 219).

Without Christ we cannot subdue a single sin or overcome the smallest temptation (*Testimonies for the Church,* vol. 4, p. 355).

You are just as dependent upon Christ, in order to live a holy life, as is the branch upon the parent stock for growth and fruitfulness. Apart from Him you have no life. You have no power to resist temptation or to grow in grace and holiness. Abiding in Him, you may flourish. Drawing your life from Him, you will not wither nor be fruitless. You will be like a tree planted by the rivers of water (*Steps to Christ*, p. 69).

In ourselves we are incapable of doing any good thing; but that which we cannot do will be wrought by the power of God in every submissive and believing soul.... It is through faith that spiritual life is begotten, and we are enabled to do the works of righteousness (*The Desire of Ages*, p. 98).

The closer you come to Jesus, the more faulty you will appear in your own eyes; for your vision will be clearer, and your imperfections will be seen in broad and distinct contrast to His perfect nature. This is evidence that Satan's delusions have lost their power; that the vivifying influence of the Spirit of God is arousing you (*Steps to Christ*, pp. 64, 65).

The sense of need, the recognition of our poverty and sin, is the very first condition of acceptance with God (*Christ's Object Lessons*, p. 152).

If the heart has been renewed by the Spirit of God, the life will bear witness to the fact. While we cannot do anything to change our hearts or to bring ourselves into harmony with God; while we must not trust at all to ourselves or our good works, our lives will reveal whether the grace of God is dwelling within us. A change will be seen in the character, the habits, the pursuits. The contrast will be clear and decided between what they have been and what they are. The character is revealed, not by occasional good deeds and occasional misdeeds, but by the tendency of the habitual words and acts (*Steps to Christ*, pp. 57, 58).

When the mind dwells upon self, it is turned away from Christ, the source of strength and life. Hence it is Satan's constant effort to keep the attention diverted from the Saviour and thus prevent the union and communion of the soul with Christ. The pleasures of the world, life's cares and perplexities and sorrows, the faults of others, or your own faults and imperfections—to any or all of these he will seek to divert the mind. Do not be misled by his devices. Many who are really conscientious, and who desire to live for God, he too often leads to dwell upon their own faults and weaknesses, and thus by separating them from Christ he hopes to gain the victory. We should not make self the center and indulge anxiety and fear as to whether we shall be saved. All this turns the soul away from the Source of our strength. Commit the keeping of your soul to God, and trust in Him. Talk and think of Jesus. Let self be lost in Him. Put away all doubt; dismiss your fears. Say with the apostle Paul, "I live; yet not I, but Christ liveth in me: and the life which I now live in the flesh I live by the faith of the Son of God, who loved me, and gave Himself for me." Galatians 2:20. Rest in God. He is able to keep that which you have committed to Him. If you will leave yourself in His hands, He will bring you off more than conqueror through Him that has loved you (*Ibid.*, pp. 71, 72).

"If Thou canst do anything, have compassion on us, and help us." How many a sin-burdened soul has echoed that prayer. And to all, the pitying Saviour's answer is, "If thou canst believe, all things are possible to him that believeth." It is faith that connects us with heaven, and brings us strength for coping with the powers of darkness. In Christ, God has provided means for subduing every sinful trait, and resisting every temptation, however strong. But many feel that they lack faith, and therefore they remain away from Christ. Let these souls, in their helpless unworthiness, cast themselves upon the mercy of their compassionate Saviour. Look not to self, but to Christ. He who healed the sick and cast out demons when He walked among men is the same mighty Redeemer today. Faith comes by the word of God. Then grasp His promise, "Him that cometh to Me I will in no wise cast out." John 6:37. Cast yourself at His feet with the cry, "Lord, I believe; help Thou mine unbelief." You can never perish while you do this—never (*Desire Ages*, page 429).

All true obedience comes from the heart. It was heart work with Christ. And if we consent, He will so identify Himself with our thoughts and aims, so blend our hearts and minds into conformity to His will, that when obeying Him we shall be but carrying out our own impulses. The will, refined and sanctified, will find its highest delight in doing His service. When we know God as it is our privilege to know Him, our life will be a life of continual obedience. Through an appreciation of the character of Christ, through communion with God, sin will become hateful to us (*Ibid.,* p. 668).

In ourselves we are incapable of doing any good thing; but that which we cannot do will be wrought by the power of God in every submissive and believing soul.... It is through faith that spiritual life is begotten, and we are enabled to do the works of righteousness (*Ibid.,* p. 98).

If you are right with God today, you are ready if Christ should come today (*Maranatha,* p. 98).

Chapter 16

Living by Faith— How to Deal With Temptation and Sin

If we are surrendered to the Holy Spirit and abiding in Jesus, we will not be sinning, for the Holy Spirit is not going to lead us to sin, nor can Satan force us to transgress while we are kept by God's power. Therefore, the only thing the devil can do is to somehow influence us to choose to step away from God. Unfortunately, he is too often successful, and we frequently find ourselves flat on our face wondering, "How did that happen?"

But let's take a closer look. Notice the following quotation from *The Ministry of Healing*: "Short and decisive are the steps that lead men down from high and holy ground to a low level" (p. 510). Before we actually commit a sin, there are definite "steps" that we take away from God. Note also that the word "steps" in this quotation is plural, so there are more than just one. Below is another quotation that gives us an excellent example of these steps. It is from *Spiritual Gifts*, volume 1, pages 20, 21. Look at the "steps" Eve took before she ate the fruit from the tree of the knowledge of good and evil.

I saw that the holy angels often visited the garden,

and gave instruction to Adam and Eve concerning their employment, and also taught them concerning the rebellion of Satan and his fall. The angels warned them of Satan, and cautioned them not to separate from each other in their employment, for they might be brought in contact with this fallen foe. The angels enjoined upon them to closely follow the directions God had given them, for in perfect obedience only were they safe. And if they were obedient, this fallen foe could have no power over them.

Satan commenced his work with Eve, to cause her to disobey. She first erred in wandering from her husband, next, in lingering around the forbidden tree, and next in listening to the voice of the tempter, and even daring to doubt what God had said—In the day that thou eatest thereof thou shalt surely die. She thought, Perhaps it does not mean just as the Lord said. She ventured to disobey. She put forth her hand, took of the fruit, and ate.

Look closely the steps she takes as the story progresses: "She *first erred* in wandering from her husband, *next*, in lingering around the forbidden tree, and *next* in listening to the voice of the tempter." These three steps, at least, were taken before "she put forth her hand, took of the fruit, and ate."

This raises an interesting question. Is it possible to do something "wrong" without sinning? Apparently so. For everything would have been OK if Eve had recognized that she had wandered away from Adam and remembered the angel's warning "not to separate from each other" and then gone back to be with him. She even would not have sinned if she had returned to Adam after she found herself around the tree and heard the snake speaking to her.

But one false step all too frequently leads to another, and the problem comes, when like Eve, we think we can handle the situation on our own. Our pride tells us we will be OK without having to run back to a godly spouse or to our spiritual brothers and sisters for counsel and encouragement to keep abiding in Jesus.

Like Eve, we may feel we don't need to run back, but let's be humble and honest. Satan is wiser and stronger than we are. If, in our own strength and wisdom, we try to meet him in *any* of his disguises, we *will* be overcome. Our only safety is in remaining in Jesus. "Humble yourselves in the sight of the Lord, and *He* will lift you up" (James 4:10). We cannot lift ourselves up or even keep ourselves in Jesus (John 15:5).

Satan comes up with unnumbered schemes trying to arouse our pride and make us think we can handle things on our own. Then, after he has caused us to sin, he continues to work on our pride, trying to keep us from going back to Jesus for cleansing and strength. "It is Satan's special device to lead man into sin, and then leave him, helpless and trembling, fearing to seek for pardon" (*Christ's Object Lessons*, p. 156).

But Jesus knows our weakness and inability. He does not want us to stay away, as our only hope is to come back to Him. Notice the following quotations from *The Desire of Ages* and *Education*:

> You have seen that all who come to Me, confessing their sins, I freely receive. Him that cometh to Me I will in nowise cast out. All who will, may be reconciled to God, and receive everlasting life. To you, My disciples, I commit this message of mercy (p. 821).

> Jesus reproved His disciples, He warned and cautioned them; but John and Peter and their brethren did not leave Him. Notwithstanding the reproofs, they chose to be with Jesus. And the Saviour did not, because of their errors, withdraw from them. He takes men as they are, with all their faults and weaknesses, and trains them for His service, if they will be disciplined and taught by Him (p. 91).

Brothers and sisters, Jesus understands our weaknesses. Let's not ever let our pride keep us away from Him. Let's confess our faults freely and ask Him for forgiveness, and grace, and for His keeping power. Did you know that by coming back to Jesus we can actually turn an apparent defeat into a victory. Notice the following quotation from *Christ's Object Lessons,* page 332:

> Do not disappoint Him who so loved you that He gave His own life to cancel your sins. He says, "Without Me ye can do nothing." John 15:5. Remember this. If you have made mistakes, you certainly gain a victory if you see these mistakes and regard them as beacons of warning. Thus you turn defeat into victory, disappointing the enemy and honoring your Redeemer.

When we step away from God and fall into sin, it can be a "beacon of warning," letting us know we are not where we want to be. Then, if we are willing to be humble and come back to Jesus, that "defeat" can be turned into a "victory"! Satan's goal is to keep us away from God. But if we let our sins and mistakes become beacons of warning and cause us to get back together with Jesus, his purpose is defeated. The question then is, Where do we really want to be? In Jesus or in sin? If we really want to be in Jesus, we must not let our pride keep us away from Him.

Better yet, God would want us to discern the "steps" that take us away from Him and let these also be "beacons of warning." By recognizing the things that tend to cause us to wander away from Him and avoiding them, or at least letting them warn us to return to His side, we can keep from sinning.

In closing, I want to share a prayer that is contained in a quotation from *Christ's Object Lessons*, which, together with the thoughts above, are what have made Christianity work for me.

> No outward observances can take the place of simple faith and entire renunciation of self. But no man

can empty himself of self. We can only consent for Christ to accomplish the work. Then the language of the soul will be, Lord, take my heart; for I cannot give it. It is Thy property. Keep it pure, for I cannot keep it for Thee. Save me in spite of myself, my weak, unchristlike self. Mold me, fashion me, raise me into a pure and holy atmosphere, where the rich current of Thy love can flow through my soul (p. 159).

May God keep you, save you, and raise you up.

Appendix

Selected Ellen White Quotations on Faith

The following pages contain select quotes from Ellen White on the subject of faith. These quotations have been an inspiration to me, and I hope that you too will be blessed and encouraged by them.

"Faith is trusting God—believing that He loves us and knows best what is for our good. Thus, instead of our own, it leads us to choose His way. In place of our ignorance, it accepts His wisdom; in place of our weakness, His strength; in place of our sinfulness, His righteousness. Our lives, ourselves, are already His; faith acknowledges His ownership and accepts its blessing" (*Education,* p. 253).

"What is faith? 'The substance of things hoped for, the evidence of things not seen.' Hebrews 11:1. It is an assent of the understanding to God's words which binds the heart in willing consecration and service to God, who gave the understanding, who moved on the heart, who first drew the mind to view Christ on the cross of Calvary. Faith is rendering to God the intellectual powers, abandonment of the mind and will to God, and making Christ the only door to enter into the kingdom of heaven" (*The Ellen G. White 1888 Materials*, p. 818).

"The season of distress and anguish before us will require a faith that can endure weariness, delay, and hunger—a faith that will not faint though severely tried. The period of probation is granted to all to prepare for that time. Jacob prevailed because he was persevering and determined. His victory is an evidence of the power of importunate prayer. All who will lay hold of God's promises, as he did, and be as earnest and persevering as he was, will succeed as he succeeded. Those who are unwilling to deny self, to agonize before God, to pray long and earnestly for His blessing, will not obtain it. Wrestling with God—how few know what it is! How few have ever had their souls drawn out after God with intensity of desire until every power is on the stretch. When waves of despair which no language can express sweep over the suppliant, how few cling with unyielding faith to the promises of God.

"Those who exercise but little faith now, are in the greatest danger of falling under the power of satanic delusions and the decree to compel the conscience. And even if they endure the test they will be plunged into deeper distress and anguish in the time of trouble, because they have never made it a habit to trust in God. The lessons of faith which they have neglected they will be forced to learn under a terrible pressure of discouragement.

"We should now acquaint ourselves with God by proving His promises. Angels record every prayer that is earnest and sincere. We should rather dispense with selfish gratifications than neglect communion with God. The deepest poverty, the greatest self-denial, with His approval, is better than riches, honors, ease, and friendship without it. We must take time to pray. If we allow our minds to be absorbed by worldly interests, the Lord may give us time by removing from us our idols of gold, of houses, or of fertile lands....

"The 'time of trouble, such as never was,' is soon to open upon us; and we shall need an experience which we do not now possess and which many are too indolent to obtain. It is often the case that trouble is greater in anticipation than in reality; but this is not true of the crisis before us. The most vivid presentation cannot reach the magnitude of the ordeal. In that time of trial, every soul must stand for himself before God. 'Though Noah, Daniel, and Job' were in the land, 'as I live, saith the Lord God, they shall deliver neither son nor daughter; they shall but deliver their own souls by their righteousness.' Ezekiel 14:20.

"Now, while our great High Priest is making the atonement for us, we should seek to become perfect in Christ. Not even by a thought could our Saviour be brought to yield to the power of temptation. Satan finds in human hearts some point where he can gain a foothold; some sinful desire is cherished, by means of which his temptations assert their power. But Christ declared of Himself: 'The prince of this world cometh, and hath nothing in Me.' John 14:30. Satan could find nothing in the Son of God that would enable him to gain the victory. He had kept His Father's commandments, and there was no sin in Him that Satan could use to his advantage. This is the condition in which those must be found who shall stand in the time of trouble.

"It is in this life that we are to separate sin from us, through faith in the atoning blood of Christ. Our precious Saviour invites us to join ourselves to Him, to unite our weakness to His strength, our ignorance to His wisdom, our unworthiness to His merits. God's providence is the school in which we are to learn the meekness and lowliness of Jesus. The Lord is ever setting before us, not the way we would choose, which seems easier and pleasanter to us, but the true aims of life. It rests with us to co-operate with the agencies which Heaven employs in the work of conforming our characters to the divine model. None can neglect or defer this work but at the most fearful peril to their souls" (*The Great Controversy*, pp. 621-623).

"In the last great conflict of the controversy with Satan those who are loyal to God will see every earthly support cut off. Because they refuse to break His law in obedience to earthly powers, they will be forbidden to buy or sell. It will finally be decreed that they shall be put to death. See Revelation 13:11-17. But to the obedient is given the promise, 'He shall dwell on high: his place of defense shall be the munitions of rocks: bread shall be given him; his waters shall be sure.' Isaiah 33:16. By this promise the children of God will live. When the earth shall be wasted with famine, they shall be fed. 'They shall not be ashamed in the evil time: and in the days of famine they shall be satisfied.' Psalm 37:19. To that time of distress the prophet Habakkuk looked forward, and his words express the faith of the church: 'Although the fig tree shall not blossom, neither shall fruit be in the vines; the labor of the olive shall fail, and the fields shall yield no meat; the flock shall be cut off from the fold, and there shall be no herd in the stalls: yet I will rejoice in the Lord, I will joy in the God of my salvation' Habakkuk 3:17, 18" (*The Desire of Ages*, pp. 121, 122).

"We must now be learning the lessons of faith if we

would stand in that time of trouble which is coming upon all the world to try them who dwell upon the face of the earth. We must have the courage of heroes and the faith of martyrs.—Letter 14, January 18, 1884, to 'Brother and Sister Newton,' a lay family" (*The Upward Look*, p. 32).

"While everything moves prosperously, people think that they have faith. But when suffering, disaster, or disappointment comes, they lose heart. A faith that is dependent on circumstances or surroundings, that lives only when everything goes smoothly, is not a genuine faith" (*Christ Triumphant*, p. 107).

"Every person will live out all the faith he has" (*Testimonies for the Church*, vol. 1, p. 195).

"Every failure on the part of the children of God is due to their lack of faith" (*Patriarchs and Prophets*, p. 657).

"God will prove His people. Jesus bears patiently with them, and does not spew them out of His mouth in a moment. Said the angel: 'God is weighing His people.' If the message had been of as short duration as many of us supposed, there would have been no time for them to develop character. Many moved from feeling, not from principle and faith, and this solemn, fearful message stirred them. It wrought upon their feelings, and excited their fears, but did not accomplish the work which God designed that it should. God reads the heart. Lest His people should be deceived in regard to themselves, He gives them time for the excitement to wear off, and then proves them to see if they will obey the counsel of the True Witness" (*Testimonies for the Church*, vol. 1, pp. 186, 187).

"The unbelief and murmurings of the children of Israel illustrate the people of God now upon the earth. Many look back to them, and marvel at their unbelief and continual murmurings, after the Lord had done so much for them, in giving them repeated evidences of his love and care for them. They think that they should not have proved thus ungrateful. But some who thus think, murmur and repine at things of less consequence. They do not know themselves. God frequently proves them, and tries their faith in small things; and they do not endure the trial any better than did ancient Israel.

"Many have their present wants supplied, yet they will not trust the Lord for the future. They manifest unbelief, and sink into despondency and gloom, at anticipated want. Some are in continual trouble lest they shall come to want, and their children suffer. When difficulties arise, or when they are brought into strait places—when their faith and their love to God are tested—they shrink from the trial, and murmur at the process by which God has chosen to purify them. Their love does not prove pure and perfect, to bear all things. The faith of the people of the God of Heaven should be strong, active, and enduring—the substance of things hoped for. Then the language of such will be, Bless the Lord, O my soul, and all that is within me, bless his holy name; for he hath dealt bountifully with me. Self-denial is considered by some to be real suffering. Depraved appetites are indulged. And a restraint upon the unhealthy appetite would lead even many professed Christians to now start back, as though actual starvation would be the consequence of a plain diet. And, like the children of Israel, they would prefer slavery, diseased bodies, and even death, rather than to be deprived of the flesh-pots. Bread and water is all that is promised to the remnant in the time of trouble" (*The Spirit of Prophecy*, vol. 1, pp. 223, 224).

"Our greatest need is faith in God. When we look on the dark side we lose our hold on the Lord God of Israel. As the heart is opened to fears and conjectures, the path of progress is hedged up by unbelief. Let us never feel that God has forsaken His work.

"There must be less talking unbelief, less imagining that this one and that one is hedging up the way. Go forward in faith; trust the Lord to prepare the way for His work. Then you will find rest in Christ. As you cultivate faith and place yourselves in right relation to God and by earnest prayer brace yourselves to do your duty you will be worked by the Holy Spirit. The many problems that are now mysterious you may solve for yourselves by continued trust in God. You need not be painfully indefinite because you are living under the guidance of the Holy Spirit. You may walk and work in confidence.

"We must have less faith in what we can do and more faith in what the Lord can do for us, if we will have clean hands and pure hearts. You are not engaged in your own work; you are doing the work of God.

"More love is needed, more frankness, less suspicion, less evil thinking. We need to be less ready to blame and accuse. It is this that is so offensive to God. The heart needs to be softened and subdued by love. The strengthless condition of our people results from the fact that their hearts are not right with God. Alienation from Him is the cause of the burdened condition of our institutions" (*Testimonies for the Church*, vol. 7, pp. 211, 212).

"There is no limit to the missionary work to be done in fulfilling this commission, and yet because of a lack of faith on the part of God's people, the work has often come almost to a standstill. The lack of any record of work accomplished in some lands testifies to the fact that many of those who have claimed to believe the truth have not revealed their faith by their works" (*Australian Union Conference Record*, October 14, 1907).

"The means in our possession may not seem to be sufficient for the work; but if we will move forward in faith, believing in the all-sufficient power of God, abundant resources will open before us. If the work be of God, He Himself will provide the means for its accomplishment. He will reward honest, simple reliance upon Him. The little that is wisely and economically used in the service of the Lord of heaven will increase in the very act of imparting. In the hand of Christ the small supply of food remained undiminished until the famished multitude were satisfied. If we go to the Source of all strength, with our hands of faith outstretched to receive, we shall be sustained in our work, even under the most forbidding circumstances, and shall be enabled to give to others the bread of life" (*The Desire of Ages*, p. 371).

"We need to look heavenward in faith. We are not to be discouraged because of apparent failure, nor should we be disheartened by delay" (*The Ministry of Healing*, p. 200).

"God Himself was working out His plan, and all that His servant [Elijah] could do was to pray on in faith and await the time for decided action" (*Prophets and Kings*, p. 133).

"The testimony of the word of God is against this ensnaring doctrine of faith without works. It is not faith that claims the favor of Heaven without complying with the conditions upon which mercy is to be granted, it is presumption; for genuine faith has its foundation in the promises and provisions of the Scriptures" (*The Great Controversy*, p. 472).

"God in His providence brought the Hebrews into the mountain fastnesses before the sea, that He might manifest His power in their deliverance and signally humble the pride of their oppressors. He might have saved them in any other way, but He chose this method in order to test their faith and strengthen their trust in Him. The people were weary and terrified, yet if they had held back when Moses bade them advance, God would never have opened the path for them. It was "by faith" that "they passed through the Red Sea as by dry land." Hebrews 11:29. In marching down to the very water, they showed that they believed the word of God as spoken by Moses. They did all that was in their power to do, and then the Mighty One of Israel divided the sea to make a path for their feet.

"The great lesson here taught is for all time. Often the Christian life is beset by dangers, and duty seems hard to perform. The imagination pictures impending ruin before and bondage or death behind. Yet the voice of God speaks clearly, 'Go forward.' We should obey this command, even though our eyes cannot penetrate the darkness, and we feel the cold waves about our feet. The obstacles that hinder our progress will never disappear before a halting, doubting spirit. Those who defer obedience till every shadow of uncertainty disappears and there remains no risk of failure or defeat, will never obey at all. Unbelief whispers, 'Let us wait till the obstructions are removed, and we can see our way clearly;' but faith courageously urges an advance, hoping all things, believing all things" (*Patriarchs and Prophets*, p. 290).

"In His Sermon on the Mount, Christ taught His disciples precious lessons in regard to the necessity of trusting in God. These lessons were designed to encourage the children of God through all ages, and they have come down to our time full of instruction and comfort. The Saviour pointed His followers to the birds of the air as they warbled their carols of praise, unencumbered with thoughts of care, for 'they sow not, neither do they reap.' And yet the great Father provides for their needs. The Saviour asks, 'Are ye not much better than they?' Matthew 6:26. The great Provider for man and beast opens His hand and supplies all His creatures. The birds of the air are not beneath His notice. He does not drop the food into their bills, but He makes provision for their needs. They must gather the grains He has scattered for them. They must prepare the material for their little nests. They must feed their young. They go forth singing to their labor, for 'your heavenly Father feedeth them.' And 'are ye not much better than they?' Are not you, as intelligent, spiritual worshipers, of more value than the birds of the air? Will not the Author of our being, the Preserver of our life, the One who formed us in His own divine image, provide for our necessities if we but trust in Him?" (*Steps to Christ*, p. 123).

"God's blessings are not bestowed upon men independent of human effort. We see this principle illustrated in the natural world. God has given us the earth with its treasures. He causes it to bring forth food for man and beast, he sends the recurring seasons, he gives the sunshine, the dew, and the rain; yet man is required to act his part; he must co-operate with God's plan by diligent, painstaking effort.

The plough must break up the soil, the seed must be sown, the field must be tilled, or there will be no harvest.

"So in the spiritual world. All that we possess, whether of talents, of influence, or of means, is of God; we can accomplish nothing without divine aid. Yet we are not released from the necessity of effort. While salvation is the gift of God, man has a part to act in the carrying out of the plan of redemption. God has chosen to use men as his instruments, to employ human agencies in the accomplishment of his purposes. He has ordained to unite divine power with human endeavor, in the work of saving souls. Thus we become laborers together with God. We have a grand and important work, because it is a part of God's great plan for the redemption of man. It is a high honor bestowed upon finite beings thus to co-operate with the Majesty of heaven" (*The Review and Herald*, December 7, 1886).

"Soon after this I had another dream. I seemed to be sitting in abject despair, with my face in my hands, reflecting like this: If Jesus were upon earth, I would go to Him, throw myself at His feet, and tell Him all my sufferings. He would not turn away from me, He would have mercy upon me, and I should love and serve Him always. Just then the door opened, and a person of beautiful form and countenance entered. He looked upon me pityingly and said: 'Do you wish to see Jesus? He is here and you can see Him if you desire to do so. Take everything you possess and follow me.'

"I heard this with unspeakable joy, and gladly gathered up all my little possessions, every treasured trinket, and followed my guide. He led me to a steep and apparently frail stairway. As I commenced to ascend the steps, he cautioned me to keep my eyes fixed upward, lest I should grow dizzy and fall. Many others who were climbing up the steep ascent fell before gaining the top.

"Finally we reached the last step and stood before the door. Here my guide directed me to leave all the things that I had brought with me. I cheerfully laid them down; he then opened the door and bade me enter. In a moment I stood before Jesus. There was no mistaking that beautiful countenance. Such a radiant expression of benevolence and majesty could belong to no other. As His gaze rested upon me, I knew at once that He was acquainted with every circumstance of my life and all my inner thoughts and feelings.

"I tried to shield myself from His gaze, feeling unable to endure His searching eyes, but He drew near with a smile, and, laying His hand upon my head, said: 'Fear not.' The sound of His sweet voice thrilled my heart with a happiness it had never before experienced. I was too joyful to utter a word, but, overcome with ineffable happiness, sank prostrate at His feet. While I was lying helpless there, scenes of beauty and glory passed before me, and I seemed to have reached the safety and peace of heaven. At length my strength returned, and I arose. The loving eyes of Jesus were still upon me, and His smile filled my soul with gladness. His presence filled me with holy reverence and an inexpressible love.

"My guide now opened the door, and we both passed out. He bade me take up again all the things I had left without. This done, he handed me a green cord coiled up closely. This he directed me to place next my heart, and when I wished to see Jesus, take from my bosom and stretch it to the utmost. He cautioned me not to let it remain coiled for any length of time, lest it should become knotted and difficult to straighten. I placed the cord near my heart and joyfully descended the narrow stairs, praising the Lord and joyfully telling all whom I met where they could find Jesus. This dream gave me hope. The green cord represented faith to my mind, and the beauty and simplicity of trusting in God began to dawn upon my benighted soul" (*Early Writings*, pp. 79-81).

"A belief that does not lead to obedience is presumption" (*Thoughts from the Mount of Blessings*, p. 146).

"But faith is in no sense allied to presumption. Only he who has true faith is secure against presumption. For presumption is Satan's counterfeit of faith. Faith claims God's promises, and brings forth fruit in obedience. Presumption also claims the promises, but uses them as Satan did, to excuse transgression. Faith would have led our first parents to trust the love of God, and to obey His commands. Presumption led them to transgress His law, believing that His great love would save them from the consequence of their sin. It is not faith that claims the favor of Heaven without complying with the conditions on which mercy is to be granted. Genuine faith has its foundation in the promises and provisions of the Scriptures" (*The Desire of Ages*, p. 126).

.